Uniquely **Australian**
A wild food cookbook

Vic Cherikoff

Uniquely Australian
A wild food cookbook

The beginnings of an Australian bushfood cuisine

Vic Cherikoff

Bush Tucker Supply Australia Pty Ltd

Published and distributed in Australia
by Bush Tucker Supply Australia Pty Ltd
ACN 003 355 753
482 Victoria Rd, Gladesville
P.O. Box B103 Boronia Park NSW 2111
Australia. 02 817 1060

Produced by Vic Cherikoff
Food styling and photography: Sanja Zemljacenko and
Vic Cherikoff
Desktop publishing consultant: Thomas MacKenzie

First printed in 1992
Reprinted in softcover 1994

© Bush Tucker Supply Australia Pty Ltd 1992
ISBN 0 646 07470 9

All rights reserved. No part of this publication may be reproduced, stored in a retrieval system or transmitted in any form or by any means, electronic, mechanical, photocopying, recording or otherwise, without the prior written permission of the publisher.

Proudly produced and printed in Australia

Travel Australia with your eyes and ears open
and it is impossible **not** to see or hear the
country crying out from abuse. We are from the land
yet are lead to believe we are independent from it.
The emergence of an Australian cuisine,
the growing acceptance of bushfoods and their
production in Enrichland Polyculture systems
(an ecologically sustainable agriculture)
may help all Australians make ties with the land.
We can all benefit.
We just need to care enough.

Contents

Preface 9

Introduction 14

Bush Cooking 22

Home Cooking 37

Fine dining 69

Sweet things 121

Bushfood glossary 189

Recipe index 199

Ingredient index 201

Menu ideas 203

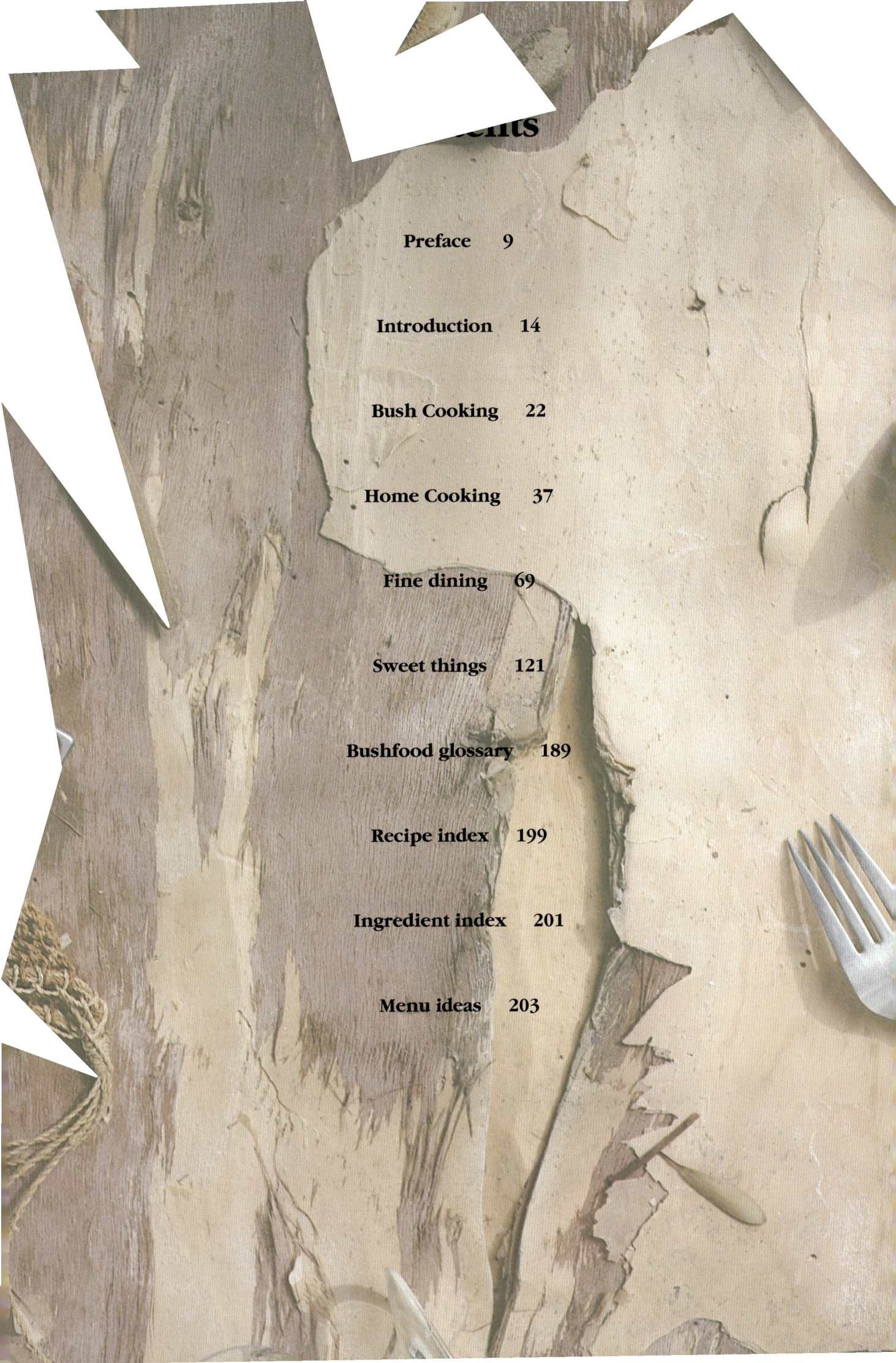

Preface

We are living in very exciting times. Most of us travel further in one year and know more people than our great grandparents did in their whole lifetimes. We are now exposed to more new ideas and more facts about world events than were our parents and our young are even learning new ways of viewing written words i.e. as screenfuls of conceptual information. Our accelerated methods of learning and information exchange means that the food industry discovers new trends, new products and new applications in hours or days not years or generations. For Australians, the post-industrial age offers huge potential. We have an emerging 'Australia' industry where our home-grown food resources are managed as a cohesive unit of Australian products in presentations to a hungry international market. These products are perceived as clean, green, fresh and of high quality and distinctive because of their Australian nature. Yet these are *exotic* products!

Authentically Australian gourmet foods which are indigenous to this country are now emerging as a significant force in the marketplace. Unlike some manufactured edibles on the market, bushfoods are closer to nature than chemistry and distinctively different in their range of appealing tastes. We can now further differentiate menus and products in Australian establishments from those found anywhere else in the world. Bushfoods and products made from them, are filling niches throughout the food, tourism, hospitality and education industries and are ecologically friendly and culturally relevant foods which give a new meaning to being Australian.

The intrinsic qualities of bushfoods provide another marketing edge. Some bushfoods can parallel the wild rice currently collected by Canadian Indians and aimed at the gourmet end of the food industry. Obviously, harvesting 'wild quality' foods from pristine environments cannot fill even the current demand for bushfoods and so an ecologically sustainable, mixed system farming method has been developed to meet market needs. This system, called Enrichland Polyculture™, is yielding produce which falls under the accepted classifications of organic and additionally, requires another category termed 'native quality'. This reflects not only the products' indigenous Australian nature but their wild characteristics which include ecological resilience, geographical suitability, high nutritional density. Some bushfoods also exhibit a protective effect against diseases of civilisation for example, diabetes and others may be useful as foods for endurance sport athletes due to their sustained energy release.

The range of bushfoods featured in this book is primarily that commercially available through an increasing number of retail outlets around the country as well as by mail order from Bush Tucker Supply Australia in Sydney. In a matter of years, we are set to create and enshrine in culinary tradition, an authentic Australian cuisine. It will be based upon ingredients native to this country, integrated into a multi-cultural food framework and include some Aboriginal cooking methods modified for the commercial kitchen. The tastes will reflect the vast outback, dense woodlands, lush rainforests, sweeping coastlines, sophisticated cities and quaint rural communities as well as the valuable natural and human resources of black and white Australians. Australia has a flavour and its a wild one!

Vic Cherikoff

Acknowledgements

This book could not have been compiled without the efforts of two groups of Australians: Firstly, the Aborigines, whose culture and lifestyle so suited this country and was so enduring in time that we can have access to a wide range of bushfoods even after 200 years of land abuse by Europeans. Secondly, the chefs, cooks, food buffs, writers and promoters who either contributed directly or shared ideas and discoveries about their experiences with bushfoods or promoted the concept embodied in this book. Without their efforts Australian bushfoods would still only be fodder for stock and I know many of them share my view that the development of an Australian cuisine is a strong statement of chauvinism and a timely multi-cultural merger of the resources of black and white Australians.

This book captures in time the recipes and ideas of Jean-Paul Bruneteau, John Downes, Andrew Fielke, Pierre Masse, Stephen Pashley, Alistair Punshon, Juleigh and Ian Robins, Scott Webster and Sanja Zemljacenko.

Jean-Paul Bruneteau contributed his recipe (see page 90) for the bunya nut pie recognising that vegetarians were all too often ignored in restaurant menus. This recipe can easily be adapted to the many native herbs and spices instead of the exotic ones.

There was a sign over the work space of the Melbourne bakery then run by natural tucker baker, **John Downes**, declaring 'wild science' was afoot and to watch John work, there must have been magic about too. John's face could suddenly disappear into a bowl of pastry mix to make sure the spices were strong enough or to check the condition of the sour dough. The technique was wild, the outcome had to be tasted to confirm the art. See pages 58, 166.

Since first introducing **Andrew Fielke** to bushfoods in the 1980s, he has continued to make a name for himself as a bushfood chef, educator and restaurateur. The Red Ochre Grill in Adelaide has won many awards in South Australia and Andrew's Head Chef from the Adelaide Red Ochre has recently opened a franchise in Cairns. Andrew's parochial recipes in this book utilise some of his State's unique resources and contribute to the ideal of a regionalised Australian cuisine. Refer to pages 70, 76, 98, 122, 140, 142, 154, 184.

Pierre Masse contributed from his experience in chocolate confiture. A lecturer at the Ryde School of TAFE, Pierre is exposing the use of bushfoods to the future young chefs and food service personnel who will be well-placed to further the development of Australian cuisine. Refer to pages 178, 179, 180.

Now ensconced in Brisbane's Gazebo Hotel, chef **Stephen Pashley** continues to present his style of bushfood cuisine. Stephen's concept of the traditional English bread and butter pudding as a wild food flavoured, up-market restaurant dessert and his preparation of char-grilled crocodile with a wattle sauce are well worth reproducing. Refer to pages 78, 82, 86, 88, 102, 124, 138.

For many years, **Alistair Punshon**, caterer, restaurateur and chef at the Metropolitan Brasserie in Bendigo, Victoria, has very successfully presented Australian cuisine to the diners of Hong Kong. Alistair's contributions reflect his chauvinism and his international experience. Refer to pages 38, 72, 74, 94, 126, 128, 130, 132, 136.

In Victoria, **Juleigh and Ian Robins** assisted the development of the bushfood industry in the early years and now specialise in wholesaling their manufactured bushfood cakes and preserves. Their culinary skills, hard work, enthusiasm and generosity have done much for the bushfood cause. Refer to pages 40, 41, 56, 62, 96, 146, 158, 160.

International chef, **Scott Webster**, has promoted bushfoods overseas both, through his own company, Australian Culinary Consultants and as consultant chef to the Australian Meat and Livestock Corporation, Australian Dairy Corporation and several other primary producer groups. Pairing native Australian ingredients and cooking methods with other Australian produce, Scott is developing his version of what he calls 'Cuisine Unique'. Thanks to Scott's work and the support of the AMLC, many overseas diners have been experiencing our developing food culture before most Australians even know of its existence. Refer to pages 80, 84, 92, 100, 104, 106, 108, 110, 112, 114, 116, 118, 120, 144.

Sanja Zemljacenko was instrumental in the production of this book. Her cooking skills and predilection for desserts produced many of the wholefood recipes presented. Sanja's artistic flair is also evident in many of the photographs as she helped me arrange and rearrange props, lighting angles and dishes. Sanja also assailed her taste buds with many of my creations and subtly resurrected a few which 'needed work'. Her assistance in consuming most of the photographic subjects proved their worth as recipes and meals. Refer to pages 54, 162, 168, 170, 172, 174, 176.

The remaining dishes were my creations or were bushfood modifications of existing recipes pulled from the culinary ether. Refer to pages 29, 30, 32, 34, 42, 43, 44, 46, 48, 50, 52, 54, 60, 64, 66, 134, 148, 149, 150, 152, 156, 164, 181, 182, 184, 186.

A book of this nature is always a collaborative production effort and there are many other people to whom I am grateful for their assistance:

Thomas MacKenzie kindly contributed his computer and software and provided long hours of expert guidance through the intricacies of desktop publishing. Thomas also assisted in the production of the page designs and final drafts.

Sophie Nerucci organised most of the photographic processing. Jane Southan helped in the early stages in typing much of the manuscript. Carole Baillargeon assisted with some of the editing. Many other friends tolerated my scrounging for props and recipe ideas and urged me on by constantly asking "How's the book going?"

On the financial side of the production, I thank Tim Kelf and the Australian Meat and Livestock Corporation for his support in the production of this book and for their efforts with Scott Webster, in pairing bushfoods with domestic meats and promoting an Australian native cuisine to the world. I wait for the day when the AMLC is directly involved in the marketing and promotion of our more ecologically appropriate native meats as well.

Qantas Airways also assisted in providing international exposure for bushfoods and Australian cuisine both through their use of bushfoods for their in-flight menus and by their sponsorship during promotions in Asia.

Finally, this second printing was facilitated by the managerial skills of my business partner in Bush Tucker Supply Australia, Bradley Field, who now shares the worries and dreams of growing the bushfood industry.

Introduction

One advantage of writing this book is the opportunity to present a history of the gestation of the bushfood industry up to the middle of 1994. My hope is that in the writing, the history does not appear too immodest as I describe my own involvement. To date, nothing would have been achieved were it not for the combined efforts of those previously acknowledged as well as those credited in my previous book, The Bushfood Handbook.

From the time of the European invasion of Aboriginal Australia up to the mid 1980s, there have been no national culinary landmarks in Australian gastronomy; not a single dish which is proudly and identifiably Australian; nor any attempt to create a discernable food culture. Chefs trained in culinary schools around Australia still learn the techniques of world cuisines and apply their skills to non-Australian ingredients. The bicentennial year of 1988 has come and gone and it appears that meat pies, vegemite, pumpkin scones, lamingtons and beer are the only offerings alleging to be Australian. Even the pavlova is concurrently claimed as theirs by New Zealanders. Two hundred years, 'Mediterrasian' cooking techniques, ingredients and combinations and no hint of an authentic Australian cuisine.

A uniquely Australian food culture can only be based upon foods indigenous to this country. The ingredients should be recognisably Australian and the dishes using them should elicit a feeling of nationalistic pride. Spices make Indian cuisines. What would Italian food be without pasta, garlic, tomato and basil? Chilli features in many tropical and aridland cuisines and high fat and starchy foods are central to the dishes of cold climate cultures. Without native Australian foods, where is the difference between local offerings and those from other countries? The flavours and even the names, for example, wattle, kurrajong, bunya, riberry, paperbark, roo and emu are as Australian as Aboriginal art or the verse of Banjo Paterson.

The possibility of an Australian cuisine first appeared in 1983. My part-time business of supplying what became the first bushfood restaurant in Australia began as a casual offer of supply. The owners of the now defunct eatery, Rowntrees The Australian Restaurant in Sydney did not take long to appreciate the potential of bushfoods, even though most of their initial 'wild' foods were collected from Sydney's street trees and urban backyards. The chef, Jean-Paul Bruneteau, with his apprentices, Matthew Deans and Junette Saskia and assisted by Hilary Wright then of the Egg Board, were instrumental in concocting several now near famous dishes. Wattleseed ice-cream and rolled wattle pavlova along with kangaroo and quandong sauce or barbequed emu sausages and bush tomato chutney, are unmistakably Australian and could certainly be candidates for national dishes. Many of the recipes in this book could be other contenders.

Interestingly, many indigenous ingredients although not recognised as such, are already well established in the mainstream food industry. From the sea; shellfish, crustaceans, bony fish, stingray and shark commonly grace our tables. Among these, Coffin Bay scallops, Top End barramundi and Sydney rock oysters among many others, regionalise some restaurant offerings. Field-shot kangaroo, farmed emu and crocodile meats are generally freely available and other meats from magpie and Cape Barren geese, mutton birds and sea snakes are available in various quantities and in different markets. As for plant foods, our native flora of 25,000 species is represented by macadamia nuts developed as a plantation species in Hawaii. From the insect world and for particular events, witjuti grubs are occasionally promoted as uniquely Australian but more often for their shock value than for their real worth as Aboriginal delicacies. Furthermore, they are usually even de-Aboriginalised in their description as *witchetty* grubs and most Australians still think the inedible scarab beetle larvae they dig up in their gardens are or were Aboriginal food.

A few freeze-dried powders used in the early days of recipe development were left-overs from samples which I had collected to be analysed during a nutritional research program at the Human Nutrition Unit in the University of Sydney. My six years of scientific research into the nutritional composition of bushfoods yielded many discoveries: It was exciting to analyse what is now marketed as the Kakadu plum and to find and be the first to confirm the world's highest fruit source of vitamin C. The protein analysis of a range of species of wattles revealed levels higher than those in high-protein wheats. Several native nuts analysed were interesting: The bunya bunya nut was almost devoid of fat and contained very complex carbohydrates. Further work in the Unit by a number of colleagues supported the idea that the nature of the carbohydrates in bushfoods played a role in protecting Aborigines against diabetes and its complications. More recent studies on complex carbohydrates and satiety factors are suggesting that a bushfood diet may be the natural way to curb appetite and maintain an ideal weight.

It has been and still is pioneering work which attracted a constant (and much appreciated) flow of attention from the media. Other researchers analysing Kakadu plum fruits, collected by the Armed Forces' Les Hiddins (but better known now as The Bush Tucker Man), questioned our vitamin C analyses maintaining they were non-specific and wild over-estimates. My results were later substantiated and the allegations disappeared. Field workers organising the bushfood collections for our own research claimed the analysis results were not filtering back to the Aborigines who supplied the samples. In response to this criticism and also in an attempt to know more about bushfoods and traditional usage, I began to travel to many Aboriginal communities in the Northern Territory and northern Queensland. Many organisations facilitated my visits to remote areas and were instrumental in allowing me to inform communities of the results of the nutritional research and of the development of a national bushfood industry. I also made contact with many local bushfood experts around the country, many of whom now provide ecologically sustainable quantities of produce to Bush Tucker Supply Australia Pty Ltd.

There are very few restaurant chefs who consider the nutritional value of the dishes they create. There is a general belief that dining out is a hedonistic indulgence in stark contrast to healthy eating. Stand in any restaurant kitchen and watch the plates come back from the tables. It is usually the foods which are high in complex carbohydrates which are more often left on the plate and the energy-dense, high fat or sweet ingredients which are eaten. Typically, the culinary masterpieces of conventionally trained chefs are high in fat and simple sugars. They are more often meat centred, with vegetables as garnishes rather than high carbohydrate meals of a range of grains, legumes, pulses, nuts and root vegetables. Scientific evidence proves that Homo sapiens is undoubtedly an omnivorous species and our ancestors have been eating meat for two million years. These days we consume large quantities of the high fat flesh of domesticated animals and not the lean, high poly-unsaturated meat of game animals. Refined cane sugar is also ubiquitous and obviously addictive while alcohol is an integral part of fine dining. In Australia, the number of vegetarians and up-market vegetarian restaurants is small but growing and few Australians consider and apply the dietary guidelines at each meal. However, knowledge of good nutrition is becoming common and advertisements often capitalise on concepts of natural and nutritious foods. Now we only need to eat as we know and not as we do. For some time yet, if restaurant eating were a daily occurrence, youthful but obese diners would probably be dying at the table.

As we continued to explore the culinary characteristics of many bushfoods my collector network grew. More innovative chefs joined our ranks and expanded the repertoire of bushfood applications. The commercial attributes of particular species became apparent and those foods with strong and distinctly different characteristics were collected in preference to less striking foods. Some of the foods presented a few challenges. Cane sugar does not suit many bush fruits due to its own characteristics masking delicate flavours and toughening fruit flesh. Some fruits react to heat in unexpected ways, turning hard or bitter on prolonged cooking. Stainless steel cooking vessels are often necessary as aluminium can potentiate bitterness. Natural substances in some fruits appear to destroy pectin added in preserve manufacture. Flavour retention and enhancement post-processing must be addressed. Often bushfood recipes needed to be developed around the particular characteristics of the bushfood rather than simply substituting the wild ingredient for a conventional one. Bushfoods will no doubt, perplex food technologists and production engineers for many years as well as challenging the food service industry.

From its conception, Bush Tucker Supply grew slowly from a chronic lack of funds. For years, ours were like voices in the wilderness, perhaps sounding foolish with the excitement of discoveries and musings of future potentials. In August 1987, the business incorporated to become the first company to exclusively promote a uniquely Australian cuisine and supply indigenous ingredients to many sectors of the food industry. The following year my commitment matured to a full-time dependence on bushfoods. In 1993 Bush Tucker Supply P/L added the Australia suffix denoting its national character and also welcomed my new business partner, Bradley Field. Bush Tucker Supply Australia Pty Ltd is now represented by eight distributors around Australia and numerous agents who provide bushfoods to dozens of restaurants, caterers, manufacturers and a wide variety of retail outlets. The Country Comfort Motel chain have maintained a strong commitment to the bushfood movement since 1990. Each of their motel restaurants features what they have called Australiana fare and continues to use bushfoods as a promotion of the company's Australian nature. Qantas and Ansett include bushfoods on their in-flight menus and other airlines are occasionally using the products to promote Australia as a tourist destination. The concept of an Australian cuisine has been embraced by the Australian Meat and Livestock Corporation for overseas promotions of Australian meats. Many Australian chefs now routinely use bushfoods in cooking competitions including the Culinary Olympics and many awards have acknowledged the bushfood content. There are now about a dozen dedicated bushfood restaurants around the country often relying on the tourist market focusing on their local flavour. More significantly and desirably), many other establishments are simply incorporating wild foods into conventional mixed cuisine menus and using them as distinctive flavourings for representative Australian dishes.

A growing number of companies are using bushfoods in value-added products. Bushfood flavoured ice creams are being made by a number of gourmet ice cream companies and still present an enormous opportunity for any entrepreneurial mainstream ice-cream manufacturer. Wild fruits, herbs and spices are increasingly being used commercially in charcuterie, bakeries, chocolate confiture, condiments and dressings. Native herb pastas are enjoying market approval even by a number of dedicated Italian cuisine establishments. A range of bushfood preserves and vinegars are proving popular and include bush tomato chutney, spreadable Kakadu plum, spreadable rosella fruit and lemon myrtle vinegar. Native herb teas available in conventional teabags are set to impact on tea drinkers who already have a coffee alternative in the caffeine-free wattleccino (see page 181). These beverages can wash down manufactured bush puddings or sienna cakes. The list is growing each week and larger manufacturers are joining our ranks generating wider acceptance and better market penetration. The export market beckons and the scope is probably endless.

Australia has indigenous ingredients which can replace many cultivated exotics. In growing these species, agriculture can contribute to the need to preserve native ecosystems as gene banks. Australian native citrus species are used overseas as rootstocks for lemons, oranges and limes. A native cucumber could provide its innate fungal resistance to genetically similar cultivated cucumbers and nearly double their commercial production per hectare and lessen the use of fungicides. However, for the food industry, most of the interest lies in the distinctly different fruits, nuts, seeds, vegetables and meats unique to Australian cuisine. Bushfood flavours defy description even by comparison to combinations of familiar tastes. New terms will be needed to describe the bushfoods selected for commercialisation. Already, the repertoire of over three dozen bushfoods and bushfood products currently available represents a significant contribution to world food. Broadening the range of bushfoods further, expands the potential of Australian cuisine.

To date, most of the supplies of bushfoods come from amenity plantings with a growing number of farmers and Aboriginal communities establishing mixed species plantations of bushfoods, medicines and timber trees. The potential for farming our cities and towns is significant since local councils and government authorities continue to use native plants to landscape public areas. Bushfoods can be harvested close to transport, processing and storage facilities, although questions of pollution and chemical contamination need to be considered. It should be apparent that with the cost of freight and labour in Australia, it is uneconomic to harvest outback bushland where foods are even more scarce now than in traditional times. This protects what remains of our disappearing bushlands from would-be commercial foragers but should add to calls for the preservation of wild areas as genetic material for the future. Many wilderness areas could be subtly tapped for their genetic resources and earn income to cover their own management costs.

Along with the strengthened environmental movement in recent years and concepts such as ecologically sustainable agriculture, the production of all our food is changing. Farmers affected by past inappropriate land management and the vagaries of the Australian climate are becoming more receptive to concepts of diversification. It is possible to integrate bushfood farming into good farm practice. Shade and shelter belts as well as soil stabilisation plantings can use locally adapted native seed and fruit bearing species. Passive farming of kangaroos and emus has yet to be established as economically viable although time will reveal the possibilities. Land holders are referring to organic methods, permaculture and bio-dynamic farming. The term Enrichland Polyculture™ specifically refers to bushland (often rehabilitated) which is enriched with a wide range of carefully selected bushfood species which are local to the area. A new system of food classification is beginning with wild quality or native quality referring to different degrees of agricultural manipulation of the species. Indigenous game animals suitably managed and wild harvested could be promoted as being of wild quality and superior in character to captive reared 'game' meats. Produce from Enrichland Polyculture systems, designed using companion and confusion planting methods and concentrating on local species would have natural quality. The production and export of bushfoods provides Australians with a unique opportunity. The bushfood industry is free of international competition yet foreign markets are hungry for produce free of pesticides, artificial fertilisers, chemical additives and the effects of disasters like Chernobyl.

There are threats to our environment which involve bushfoods. Extractive industries reduce genetic diversity and are never sustainable. Ignoring our resources can be as threatening as over-using them. Unless Australia's arid lands are converted from the production of domestic animals to more appropriate native ones, desertification will continue to spread. It is irresponsible to squander our limited natural wealth through ignorance of the facts. Opponents to this necessity have not yet woken up to the fact that there is no choice. If Australians choose to eat meat then it should be produced in an ecologically sustainable way. Domestic animal production has been falling in recent years with farmers moving off lands made unproductive by past land management practices. Rearing sheep, cattle and other domesticates is not sustainable or appropriate in much of Australia. Governments must act to facilitate the transition from captive rearing to the passive farming of those native animals which are suitable for meat production. Several species of kangaroo are being killed as pests and their carcasses wasted instead of the species managed as a uniquely Australian resource. Emus are being intensively farmed and their wild quality suffers. Passive farming of emus should be researched so that the birds live in their natural habitats until humanely harvested.

The true modern Australian cuisine (one which has a past) is more than just a unique set of native ingredients. It also includes many Aboriginal culinary techniques some of which have withstood the tests of nearly a decade and are being applied and adapted to contemporary needs in the commercial kitchen. Traditional preparative methods often use paperbark, fragrant timbers and aromatic fruits and herbs, for introducing a range of characteristically Australian flavours to products and finished dishes. Bushfood cuisine also uses portions of native foods which are largely ignored in this country. Perhaps adoption of the Aboriginal appreciation of fish offal as a delicacy and its specialised preparation may soon yield up-market offerings at innovative restaurants.

The use of bushfoods has a wider social role. The 1990s have seen a resurgence of pride in Aboriginality. While the standard of living of Aborigines remains well behind that of other Australians, Aboriginal culture is still able to hold claim to being the oldest continuous living culture in the world. The end of the century may yet see bushfood and bush culture brought back into alignment for the benefit of anyone who eats. Aborigines themselves are again using bushfoods (and bush medicines) as nutritive, healing and tonic agents and as a reinforcement of their ties to the land. More and more outback communities are beginning to manage existing bushfoods and some are planting mixed systems of local species as cash crops. While harvesting bushfoods with adults, Aboriginal children learn and practice traditional ways. Techniques such as seed stripping and parching, yandying and winnowing are reinforcing Aboriginality while adding to earned income. Bushfoods are being collected with a renewed vigour and their nutritional contribution is rising in importance. Bushfoods are also becoming an integral part of Aboriginal presentations of their culture to the wider community. There are now even urban Aborigines conducting bush tucker tours for tourists and schools often catering the tour with purchased bushfoods. This could be developed much further. Dining out may become a bush experience in a landscaped corner of an Aboriginal restaurant garden. Food could emerge from a ground oven, an ash bed or from under a mound of coals as Aboriginal hosts share their local traditions in the same way as do the parochial family restaurants of rural Europe or the Maori communities of New Zealand. Aboriginal music, art, stories and bushfood traditions could meld into an experience unparalleled internationally. In the future, it may be possible to dine in a rainforest (this presumes rainforests survive to the future) and enjoy dishes prepared using foods from the surrounding environment. Even the restaurant could be landscaped with edible native plants. This experience could be repeated in tropical, temperate and sub-temperate rainforests. Similarly, restaurants in the deserts or the high country, in forests, woodlands or grasslands or those around our coastline could offer regional specialities to make touring this country a gastronomic exploration to match the splendour of our natural vistas.

Australian cuisine has been conceived. It is still in its infancy but it is here to stay. There is a growing obligation amongst bushfood users to maintain their integrity when creating new products and to do justice to the flavours of primary ingredients. There is little point in producing dishes which could have been made with conventional ingredients but sold as bushfood. Currently being marketed are a witchetty grub soup with nearly no grubs and a flavourless quandong jam which could easily be made without the quandong. Another potential pitfall is in blending flavours into indiscernable concoctions before the individual tastes have become widely recognisable. The bushfood industry must focus on quality products rather than on tokenism since only the former acknowledges the legacy of the Culture of the Land and contributes to the development of a genuine Australian cuisine.

One possible scenario which may be less than five years away, is that Australian cuisine will be based upon an increasing range of bushfoods which have been produced in sustainable, biologically diverse and often passive agricultural systems, without noxious artificial chemicals. In restaurants and in the home, these high quality foods will be combined using traditional Aboriginal techniques as well as modern culinary skills by cooks who unconsciously apply the Australian dietary guidelines for good nutrition and health. Then, those of us in this hypothetical lucky country would certainly be uniquely Australian.

Uniquely Australian

Sydney Salad

4 cups of mesclun salad mix including rocket, raddichio, whitlof, coral and coz lettuces, cresses, sprouts and petals
1 egg yolk
salt
1/2 teaspoon mustard
1/4 teaspoon ground lemon myrtle
40ml lemon myrtle vinegar
125ml macadamia nut oil
1/2 cup croutons
1 tablespoon butter
1 teaspoon ground mountain pepper
1/2 cup shaved parmesan cheese
1 tablespoon akudjura
1 avocado
8 red or yellow baby tomatoes
30g cold cured smoked kangaroo or emu prosciutto (optional)
oil for frying

With the egg yolk, mustard, vinegar and oil all at room temperature, combine the yolk, salt, mustard, vinegar and ground lemon myrtle in a stainless steel mixing bowl.
While whisking briskly, add the macadamia nut oil by the tablespoon at first then more quickly later. Whisk to a thick white mayonnaise, thinning to a dressing with a little more vinegar, if necessary.
Melt the butter in a small saucepan, remove from heat and add the croutons. Toss to coat them with the butter and then sprinkle with the mountain pepper. Set aside.
Slice the prosciutto into slivered pieces and sauté in a small amount of oil until crisp. Drain on an absorbent towel.

Arrange each serve of salad in the middle of a large plate and add the avocado slices or alternatively, use hard-boiled egg halves. Drizzle the salad with the lemon myrtle dressing. Portion the kangaroo, scattering around and over the salad. Sprinkle each plate with a generous amount of akudjura. Finish with the croutons and shaved parmesan. Garnish with the tomatoes for colour.

*This recipe is dedicated to the Sydney Olympic effort and the culinary strength of the Sydney food scene.
It also recognises the value of signature dishes as a marketing tool.
The Caesar, Waldorf and Greek salads on offer around the world may be different versions of their original recipe.
However, customers know roughly what to expect.
This is the reason for their popularity and almost ubiquitous global presence on restaurant menus.*

Bush cooking

The art of cooking with wood fires is still a part of Aboriginal tradition but it should be more natural to all Australians. Has the time gone when a billy and a knife made up the whole kitchen? What has happened to the Australian tradition of Waltzing Matilda which was the epitome of travelling light?

When most city folk go bush, the fossil-fuel fed stove gets loaded into the trailer as if there was no other way to prepare food without it. Even when backpacking, light-weight stoves often become 'essential' burdens. The more experienced bush traveller may still use an open fire but will usually leave some sign of their passing. In the most remote parts of the bush it is always easy to pick a 'white fellas' camp by the ring of stones around the fire as if to define it. In fact, the stones usually limit the usefulness of the fire. They preclude using hot ash at the fireside for cooking, make any food buried under the fire hard to turn and make long sections of firewood difficult to burn. It is easier to stick one end of a whole log into the fire and move it up into the fire as it burns rather than get blisters chopping wood with an axe or wasting fossil fuels on chainsaws.

At home in the backyard, open fires have been replaced with gas-fired barbeques as consumers succumb to technology whether it is progressive or not. A little thought and improvisation can modify a 44 gallon drum, cut in two lengthways and filled with sand into an almost portable raised open fire suitable for patios and balconnies.

Food is rarely cooked in naked flames. Hot coals and ash are more useful and far more versatile. Any whole food can be conveniently cooked by burying it under hot ash, sand and coals. The method is well suited for cooking small unskinned animals and reptiles, whole insects and unpeeled vegetables. Small animals often do not even need to be gutted as they cook quickly and the entrails will dry and shrink to be removed before serving. Larger foods, for example, gutted whole fish, can be baked on top of live coals or for edible titbits, live coals can be picked out and tumbled in a dish. Bogong moths are easily cooked in this way. The moths are mixed with live coals replacing the coals as they cool until the moths smell like oily, roasted nuts. Shrub seeds were traditionally parched this way before being ground to flour. The final clean-up requires the Aboriginal technique of yandying to remove the debris from the coals and ash to leave the food ready for eating or further processing.

To make an ash cooking fire set and burn enough light timber on loose ground to make a mound of hot ash and an area of heated ground under the fire. Hot ash spread on cold ground is quickly made useless for cooking as it cools and the heated ground is important for adequate cooking. When sufficient ash has been generated, usually after a good hour of burning light timbers, scoop a hollow, drop in the food and cover it up well with hot ash. The hollow should still leave heated ground as the base for the food as this heat may mean that the food will not need to be turned. It is important to get plenty of hot ash (not live coals) around the food as this excludes oxygen from around the food and reduces the chance of burning. Hot coals in direct contact with the food will spot burn the food. If only a small amount of ash has been generated or the ash and sand are not very hot, then set a light brush fire over the buried food for additional heat and lengthen the cooking time. The food item may also need to be turned over and then covered again with more hot ash.

Uniquely Australian

Wherever you cook, whether its in the backyard or the bush, the cooking area needs a little thought and planning. A ground oven trench is best placed so that an area in close proximity can be used to put hot coals removed once the rocks have been heated. Another spot will be needed to pile the hot rocks and obviously cold or wet ground is unsuitable. The coal heap should not be up-wind otherwise you will be working in smoke and heat as you build the ground oven. The rock pile should be close enough to hand to make the oven assembly convenient. Clean sand around the whole cooking area is the easiest material for covering the oven, it also looks good, reduces the fire spread risk and is useful if cooking shellfish northern Aboriginal style, that is, pressed into moist sand and steamed. It is also easy to cook small items, for example, tubers or witjuti grubs in heated sand.

In bush cooking, the use of combinations of hot ash and sand, heated rocks and live coals simplifies the utensils needed. On several open fires with a range of timbers to burn to produce ash and coals, with a billy, some paperpark, a pair of long handled tongs, gardening gloves for safety and a shovel, you can easily cook a five course meal for 20 *and* serve wattle. The most limiting items are the industrial age billies. Set in a garden landscaped with bush food plants, natural rock settings and maybe a small water garden as well, a fire can provide the focus of a backyard barbie on a balmy summer night or a warm spot to sit through a cold winter. A little experience of Aboriginal lifestyle and your swag may end up alongside the fire for most of the year and the bedroom only used when it rains!

Below: *Cooking witjuti grubs in hot ash.*

Uniquely Australian

Shellfish in sand

Any bivalved (double shelled) mollusc including pippies, mussels, cockles and clams can be cooked together in this way. Press the shellfish into moist sand, hinge uppermost. This stops the shell from opening once it is cooked and lessens the chance of grit from the fire getting inside. Once all the shellfish are lined up pile on some burning twigs and keep this light fire going for about 10 minutes. Different shellfish species will need different amounts of heat to cook. Cockles and clams have much heavier shells than pippies or mussels. In order to cook the collection of shellfish evenly, leave burning twigs over the larger shells for longer. Once all the shells appear a little charred and experience can confirm that the

shellfish inside are adequately cooked then remove any remaining burning twigs. Brush away the ash and debris using a leafy branch as a broom. Carefully pick up the hot shellfish (a piece of paperbark or a leaf makes a good plate), wipe the edge free of sand and it should open with almost no effort. If not, put it onto hot coals for a few minutes more to finish.

This traditional Aboriginal method of cooking shellfish steams the food keeping it juicy inside and imparts a delicate smoke flavour to the seafood as well.

Above Pippies and cockles about to be covered with burning twigs.
Right Cooked shellfish brushed clean with a green branch and almost ready to be served.

Uniquely Australian

Cobra or mangrove worm

Mangrove worm, shipworm or marine borer is commonly known as 'cobra' and makes a milky soup when boiled in salted fresh water. They can also be eaten raw by putting one end in your mouth and sucking in like you would with a long piece of spaghetti. Keep your lips sealed around the worm so that any crushed shellgrit on the outside of the worm can simply be wiped away once you have sucked the worm in. Cobra is a mollusc living in a calcified tube and some shell is to be expected. The flavour of the shellfish is somewhere between the manufactured chocolate mineral drink, Aktavite® and rock oysters. Cobra was moreoften a women's food and we now know it is a very good source of many minerals and particularly iron, copper and zinc.

Gracey has the skill of 'singing' mangrove worms from their logs rather than just pulling them out. One record she set was a 1.8 metre worm.

A word of caution about cooking with hot sand: Sand is the same colour whether it is very hot or stone cold. If bare skin touches hot sand severe burns can result. The hot sand sticks and because it holds heat so well it cooks your skin and makes for a very bad injury, so be warned!

Seafood on coals

A wide range of seafood can easily be turned in the coals to cook. The list includes mudcrabs, fish, sharks and stingray as well as single shelled molluscs, for example, periwinkles, nerites, vongoles and many others. Like periwinkles, the spiralled shellfish in the photograph above has a deep green coloured flesh with a strong flavour rich in minerals from the algae and plankton on which the animal feeds. Once cooked, carefully take the shells out of the fire, remember they will be very hot and hammer the shell and extract the edible portion. This particular species is so easy to find along the northern coastline of the Top End that some Aborigines call them 'beef'. Longbum is another common name.

When cooking stingray, only take animals about dinner plate size or do not eat the liver of large animals. Gut the ray, reserving the liver and keeping it cool. Cook the underside of the ray first, then while the other side is cooking, lay out the liver over the cooked flesh. Place several live coals on top of the liver and keep replacing cooled coals with live ones until the flesh and the liver are cooked. Tear or chop the cooked liver through the prepared flesh and the ray is ready to eat.

Uniquely Australian

The long supermarket

It may seem facetious but for the serious gourmand, Australian roads can be likened to a long supermarket where the keen eyed shopper can pick up a bargain in the form of fresh road kills. Please leave the pedestrians since their relatives will more often object but depending on the season, the time of day and locality, a wide range of snakes, goannas, tortoises, parrots and of course, large and small mammals can be found victim to the speeding, inattentive motorist. Your nose and common sense will advise you as to the freshness of the animal and obviously, only just-killed animals are worth eating. Often the victims will still need to be despatched since vehicles are very inefficient weapons. A small hatchet or a crow bar is a useful tool to carry for this purpose but any heavy blunt object will do. Use a short sharp blow to the back of the animals head low down to the spine. With small animals, hold the head to the ground with your boot and pull the neck to dislocate the vertebrae. Gut and cook the animal as soon as possible.

The foregoing may seem callous to those who are willing to accept the result but not to do the deed. If you choose to eat meat then take the responsibility of that decision. An animal's muscles may be called rump, T-bone, chops, racks or sirloin but the inescapable truth is that it is still a part of what was once a living organism. We all kill to eat and in our own way and in our own time we are all food for someone or something.

Uniquely Australian

Fresh water python or file snake is a common food for northern Australian Aborigines. The meat tastes very similar to crocodile which is often described as a fishy chicken.

All reptiles are protected throughout Australia. They play a valuable role in their ecologies and should be admired from a distance but left alone.

The only time they could find their way onto the menu is if they are found dead on the road and are still fresh enough to eat.

The best way to cook a snake, eel or any lizard is by burying it whole under hot ash and then covering it with coals. Roasting goanna on top of an open fire will toughen the meat making for a hard chew. However, this latter method of preparation is recommended in a survival situation where one meal may have to last a long time.

Uniquely Australian

Johnny cakes

To make 1 large Johnny cake

2 cups flour
½ cup powdered milk
1 teaspoon baking powder
2 teaspoons sieved ash from a previous fire
flavourings (see below)
water for mixing

Sift all the dry ingredients. The ash is an excellent substitute for bread improver as it augments the action of the rising agent. Add sufficient water to take in most of the dry mix while mixing with a spoon. Use the remaining dry mix to rub the spoon clean or your hands if you began the mixing with them. Finally, briefly knead the mix to make a soft dough adding more water if necessary. The best dampers are not kneaded too much and are left to sit for about 20 minutes before cooking. Wild food flavourings for Johnny cakes include pre-boiled wattle, native pepper, lemon tea tree, lemon myrtle or native aniseed used singly or in combination. The leaves can either be chopped or ground very finely or infused and the tea used for mixing the dough.

Uniquely Australian

Beach camp crab soup

To serve 4

1 litre water
150g (1 medium sized) yam
150g cassava
1 large or 2 medium mud crabs
milk and flesh from 2 coconuts or
100ml coconut cream and ½ cup of coconut flakes
5 leaves of native pepper
½ cup seaweed, chopped finely if necessary
½ bunch warrigal greens, blanched
seasoning (salt or tamari)

To make the soup, wash and peel the yam and cassava and cut them into chip sized pieces. Add the chips, coconut flesh or flakes, coconut milk or cream, pepperleaves and seaweed to the water and bring it to the boil. Include the crab meat or the whole crab at this stage. Simmer until the yam is soft. Coarsely chop the already blanched warrigal greens and add them to the soup. Bring the soup back to a gentle boil before serving. Adjust the seasoning. Garnish each soup serve with freshly crumbled pepperleaf.

If cooking at home the crabs can be put into the freezer for an hour to kill them or scramble their brain with a knife inserted behind the eyes. The crab can then be cooked in a separate volume of boiling water, the flesh from the claws removed and added to the soup. Include the opened carapace into the soup for flavouring and remove it before service. The oils from the crab's nervous tissues will add flavour to the soup.

Alternatively, wash the crab well and boil it whole in the soup. Break up the cooked crab into the required number of pieces and leave the retrieval of the flesh to each diner. The seaweed used can be foraged or bought dried. If it is foraged, be sure it is edible. If purchased dry, soak the seaweed overnight to soften it before use.

Uniquely Australian

The warrigal green salad with the citrus tang of lemon aspen complements the crab, yam and coconut in the soup.

Barramundi out bush

To serve 2

1 whole barramundi, unscaled and ungutted

Fish fries

Carefully remove all the entrails including the swim bladder. This is the long white sack at the top of the gut cavity. Discard the gut itself and any tissues with a bile green colour. Open the wider end of the swim bladder and stuff in the fat, organs and associated tissues. Skewer the opening with a twig or sew it together with string and then fry this package in a dry skillet over medium heat. The fat inside will adequately grease the skillet. Turn the stuffed bladder often and fry until crisp on the outside. Use the fish fries simply chopped as a garnish to the cooked fish flesh or as the basis of a rich sauce, stock or soup.

Fish flesh

To cook the rest of the fish, bake the now gutted barramundi on top of hot coals. Leave the scales on and keep turning the fish as it cooks to avoid burning spots in direct contact with coals. Once cooked, lay the fish onto some fresh leaves and with a knife inserted along the backbone halve the fish and remove the bones. Lift out the cooked flesh leaving behind the skin and scales. Don't ignore the cheek which is the 'eye-fillet' of the fish. Serve on a plate of fresh leaves and garnish the fish with the chopped fish fries prepared previously.

A nutritional pairing of the starchy yam with the high taste (high oil) seafoods of barramundi and eel.

Cooking in a ground oven

Ground oven cooking is a skill which can only be learned through experience but it is one worth learning. Judging the number and size of the rocks to be heated in relation to the amount of food to be cooked is one part of the equation. The intensity of the fire and the heat put into the ground under the fire are still other variables. Then there is the mass of the food items which, if too large, will stop the food from cooking through evenly. Finally, the heat in the rocks before closing the prepared oven and the thickness of the insulating layer of earth over the oven are important.

The construction is as follows: A pit is dug to a depth of around 30 centimetres and the sides packed down so that loose soil will not fall into the hole while working around it. Build a substantial fire in the pit and on top of the fire place enough rocks to equal or be a little less than the mass of food to be cooked. Use fist-sized rocks which will hold heat and not crumble (experience again but river stones are a definite no-no). Pieces of fired bricks, conglomerate, basalt, granite and dense sandstone are among those that work well and can be reused many times. Shale, sandstock and claystone break up into tiny pieces which quickly lose their heat and add sand sized particles to the food. This latter point is not too much of a problem if you can teach your guests not to bring their teeth too close together when they chew your gritty offerings. However, it is better to choose your rocks carefully and avoid the roughage. The size of the fire and the length of time the rocks are heated affect the cook's stress levels. If suitable rocks are heated to red heat the oven can be assembled at a more leisurely pace than if less hot. However, rocks that are too hot will burn the food. Again, it is a matter of experience.

Once the rocks are heated, the oven can begin to be assembled. The food and the paperbark which will line the oven should have been prepared and be at hand. Large food items will have been sectioned to serving size although foods with the dimensions of medium sized kumara or yams can be left whole and cut once cooked.

Using long tongs, a shovel and wearing leather gardening gloves, remove all the hot rocks from the fire pit, piling all the rocks in a heap and leaving the ash and coals behind. Remove all coals from the pit but do not disturb the heated ground under the fire. This is an important point since the hot earth contributes to the cooking significantly. Once the pit is clean, line it with paperbark using large sheets for the bottom and tucking the side pieces under the bottom lining and up the sides of the pit. Put in the food and arrange the hot rocks putting smaller rocks on top of soft cooking foods and larger rocks around larger food items. Fish can be sandwiched between flat rocks. Birds can be stuffed with a hot rock to cook from the inside out.

Hot rocks nestled amongst fist-sized foods and scattered according to heat and mass.

Home cooking

The major differences between what is possible when cooking at home and up-market restaurant meals are presentation and nutrition. Generally, both types of food styles win a point each. However, a little care and flair can dress up home-cooked meals to challenge the artistry of even the five-star restaurant chef. Look at how chefs use garnishes and side dishes of vegetables, sauces and pickled fruits. Garnishes improve what dietitians know as the organo-leptic qualities of food. These are intended to tantalise the senses and stimulate appetite and are synonymous with good eating. Other attributes of good food are presentation colour, texture and of course, the aroma and taste.

The common use of cream, sugar and shortenings in restaurant food makes for high energy (but also high taste) dishes. Home cooked meals without these evil additives tend to be more nutritious. Low fat foods high in fibre do not need to be low in taste. Trim the saturated fat from meats or stick to native game meats. Prepare and eat more vegetarian dishes. Rather than using cream for flavour enhancement, try a mixture made from a little tahini blended to a cream consistency with cooked bunya nuts and soy milk. To replace stock and seasonings try a little white or dark miso (available from Asian food suppliers) with a dash of a strong infusion of wattle. Use homemade bushfood vinegars and wild fruit juices for flavourings. To challenge the flavours of high fat cooking, use herbs and spices or focus on foods with distinctive tastes. Bush foods have just the strength of character to help make nutritious meals as flavoursome as restaurant fare. Care should also be taken not to overcook vegetables and game meats should always be served no more than medium rare to preserve texture, flavour and nutritional value. A general rule when adapting recipes to include bushfoods or creating bushfood recipes, could be to consider the dietary guidelines as well as the traditional diet of our ancestors.

Carbohydrate foods which are low in fat are an excellent complement to ingredients richer in fats and should form the bulk of any meal. Flavouring carbohydrate foods could be described as the basis of vegetarian cookery and the high intake of carbohydrates may be more similar to the diet with which Homo sapiens evolved. Interestingly, many diseases of civilisation are linked to high fat and highly refined foods while complex carbohydrates appear to play a protective role. These same carbohydrates also contribute to satiety and so a bushfood diet is more filling than cultivated food.

The following recipes have been formulated with the Australian nutritional guidelines in mind. They are predominantly vegetarian and are low in fat and refined sugars. Non-vegetarian dishes use the very lean game meats of kangaroo and emu or seafood but any cuts of Australian beef and lamb, buffalo, goat or poultry trimmed of excess fat are appropriate. The main dishes are usually high in complex carbohydrates and combine ingredients selected to accent the uniquely Australian flavour of the bushfoods used.

Roo stew under a kurrajong crust

To serve 4

400g kangaroo backstrap
plain flour for dusting
bush tomatoes, ground
paprika for seasoning
oil for frying
1 onion, diced
2 cloves garlic, finely chopped
port
2 tablespoons tomato paste
meat stock
autumn or spring vegetables, diced

Chop the meat into 6cm cubes. Season the flour with ground bush tomatoes and paprika and flour the meat pieces. Heat the oil in the camp oven and toss in the floured meat and fry to seal the meat. Remove from the oven and set aside. In extra oil, sweat the onion. Add the garlic and fry until brown. Add back the meat, a splash of port, the tomato paste and cover with the meat stock.

Bring to the boil and simmer until the meat is tender adding the vegetables 20 minutes before the end. Make the kurrajong crust, cover the stew and bake to brown as follows:

Kurrajong crust

250g plain wholemeal flour
2 tablespoons kurrajong flour
125g butter
1 egg
salt
water to bind

Combine ingredients in a food processor to make a dough. Roll out to the size of the camp oven and cover the hot stew. Glaze with egg white, sprinkle on sesame seeds, refit the lid and stand the camp oven on warm coals. Cover the lid with hot coals or bake in a conventional oven at 220°C for 15 to 20 minutes.

Prawn and ginger soup

To serve 2

200g prawns, shelled
1 tablespoon butter
1 tablespoon flour
1 litre fish stock
2 teaspoons finely grated ginger
30ml white wine
60ml cream
seasonings
native pepperleaf

In a large saucepan over medium heat, melt the butter and add the flour, stirring to make the sauce base. Add the fish stock and cook to thicken. Add the grated ginger. Pour in the wine and cream and season to taste. Add the peeled prawns and poach for 1½ to 2 minutes. Remove the prawns to serving bowls, cover with the soup and liberally sprinkle on freshly ground pepperleaf.

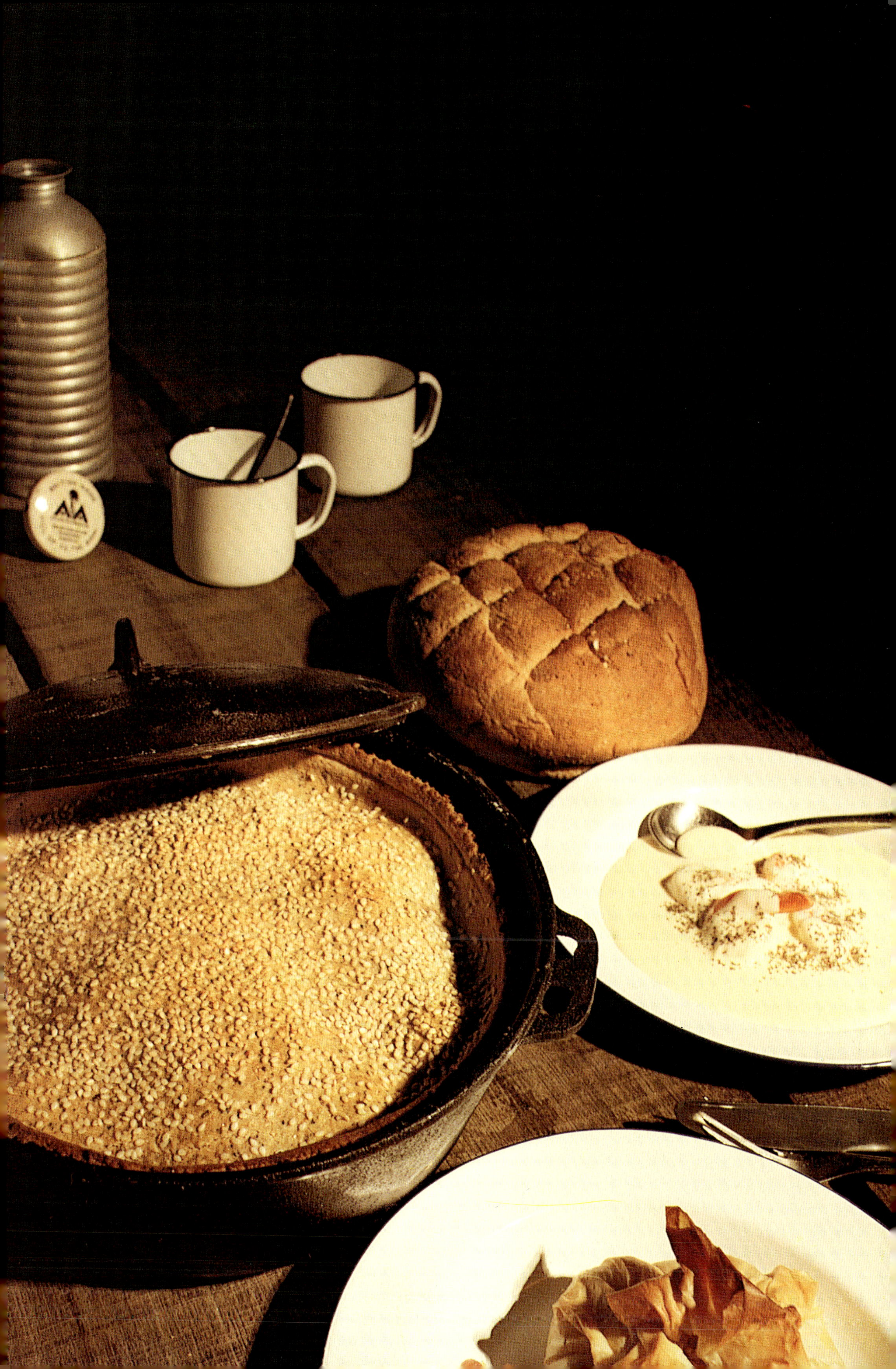

Bush tomato soup

To serve 6

**12 large ripe tomatoes
2 onions
seasonings
1 tablespoon oil
½ cup basil leaves
6 cups vegetable stock
50g bush tomatoes**

Finely chop the tomatoes, onions and basil. In a pot, heat the oil and add the chopped ingredients, frying until tender. Add the vegetable stock and seasonings. Finely chop the bush tomatoes and add these to the pot and simmer until the soup becomes thick and rich (45 to 60 minutes). Remove from heat and blend until smooth. The bush tomato flavour will strengthen with time. This soup can also be thickened to a sauce for pizzas or pasta.

Mini pizzas

To serve 6

2⅓ cups plain flour
½ cup rye flour
1 teaspoon fresh yeast
225ml tepid water
¼ tablespoon salt
½ tablespoon oil

Sift the flours and salt into a bowl. Dissolve the yeast in a little of the tepid water and mix it into the flour with the oil and the rest of the water to form a soft dough. Cover with a tea towel and allow it to rest and rise in a warm spot for 1 hour. Flatten the dough on a floured surface and roll out to ½ cm thickness. Cut into 6 cm rounds. Top with a covering of bush tomato soup, mushroom strips, sun-dried tomatoes, fetta cheese and finish with a sprinkle of ground bush tomatoes. Bake the mini pizzas at 400°C for 8 to 10 minutes.

Other toppings could include mozzarella and tasty cheeses, a range of wild and cultivated mushrooms (try fresh shitake mushrooms or wild puffballs finely chopped), corn kernels, pineapple pieces or capsicum. In South Australia, Pepperooni™ is being made from kangaroo meat and traditional pepperoni spices and is well suited to pizzas. Alternatively, smoked kangaroo or emu meat makes a good substitute for a bush bacon if it is first pan-fried in a little oil to heighten the flavour. Other pizza ingredients could include a heavy sprinkle of ground native pepper to put in a little zing or try brushing the pizza bases with lemon aspen juice before adding the other toppings.

Native herb vinegars

Some interesting native herb vinegars can be made from the twigs and leaves of lemon myrtle, native aniseed, native pepper, lemon tea tree or rainforest celery. To 1 litre of the best quality white wine vinegar, add 5 to 10g of any of the native herbs. The rainforest celery will need to be used a little more generously, about 50g. Bring the vinegar to the boil in a covered stainless steel saucepan. Reduce the heat and allow to gently simmer for 15 minutes. Pour the herb vinegar into sterilised bottles including some fresh leaves of the selected herb.

Rainforest celery

Uniquely Australian

Corn, myrtle and lime soup

1 litre water
corn kernels from 2 cobs
1 medium carrot, pieced
1 large onion, sliced
6 wild mushrooms or 1 large puffball
6 large lemon myrtle leaves
1 tablespoon tamari or low salt soy sauce
1 tablespoon lemon myrtle vinegar
1 tablespoon mirin
6 native limes

Bring the water to a boil and add the onions. Simmer for a few minutes. Add all the vegetables and the lemon myrtle. If wild mushrooms are not available use shitake mushrooms and Chinese black fungus. If dry mushrooms are used, soak before cooking. Cover and simmer for 10 to 15 minutes or until the carrots are cooked. Season with tamari, lemon myrtle vinegar and mirin. Garnish each bowl with lime halves and serve with a crusty bread.

This soup makes an excellent summer soup if served cold.

Bunya nut and pumpkin soup

1 medium butternut pumpkin
150g bunya nuts, boiled and shelled
2 large onions, chopped
1½ cups soy milk
2 tablespoons sour cream
seasoning to taste

Wash the pumpkin, cut it into a bowl size and remove the seeds. Place the cut side down onto an oiled baking tray and bake at 350°C for about 60 minutes or until soft. Scoop out the cooked flesh leaving enough to keep the bowl firm. Fry the onions until they are translucent, salting them lightly. Blend the onions, bunya nuts and pumpkin flesh to smoothness adding the soy milk to adjust the consistency. Reheat prior to serving in the pumpkin bowl and add the sour cream.to finish.

Mushroom soup

1 tablespoon oil for frying
2 large onions, chopped
1 teaspoon freshly grated ginger
3 cups assorted wild mushrooms, chopped
½ teaspoon salt
3 native pepper leaves
2 cups vegetable stock or water
2 tablespoons tahini
3 tablespoons peanut butter
200g soft tofu

Fry the onions and ginger in the oil until the onions brown. Add the mushrooms, cover and cook on a low heat, for about 10 minutes. Add the salt. In a food processor, blend the tofu in some of the stock. Add the mushrooms and process until smooth, adding stock to adjust the consistency. Pour the blended mixture into a saucepan and add the pepperleaves. Bring the soup to the boil and briskly stir in the tahini and peanut butter. Simmer for 25 minutes.

Chilled warrigal green soup

oil for frying
2 large onions, chopped
1 medium potato, chopped
1 teaspoon salt
2 native pepperleaves
2 cups coconut milk
250g warrigal greens, blanched
1 cup coconut cream
1 cup plain yoghurt

Fry the onions in the oil on a low heat. After about 10 minutes, add the potato, salt, pepperleaves and coconut milk. Boil then reduce the heat and simmer until potatoes are tender. Remove from heat and extract the pepperleaves. In a food processor, blend the soup with the warrigal greens. Whisk in the yoghurt and the coconut cream. Chill for a few hours and adjust thickness, if necessary with additional coconut milk. Serve in coconut shell bowls.

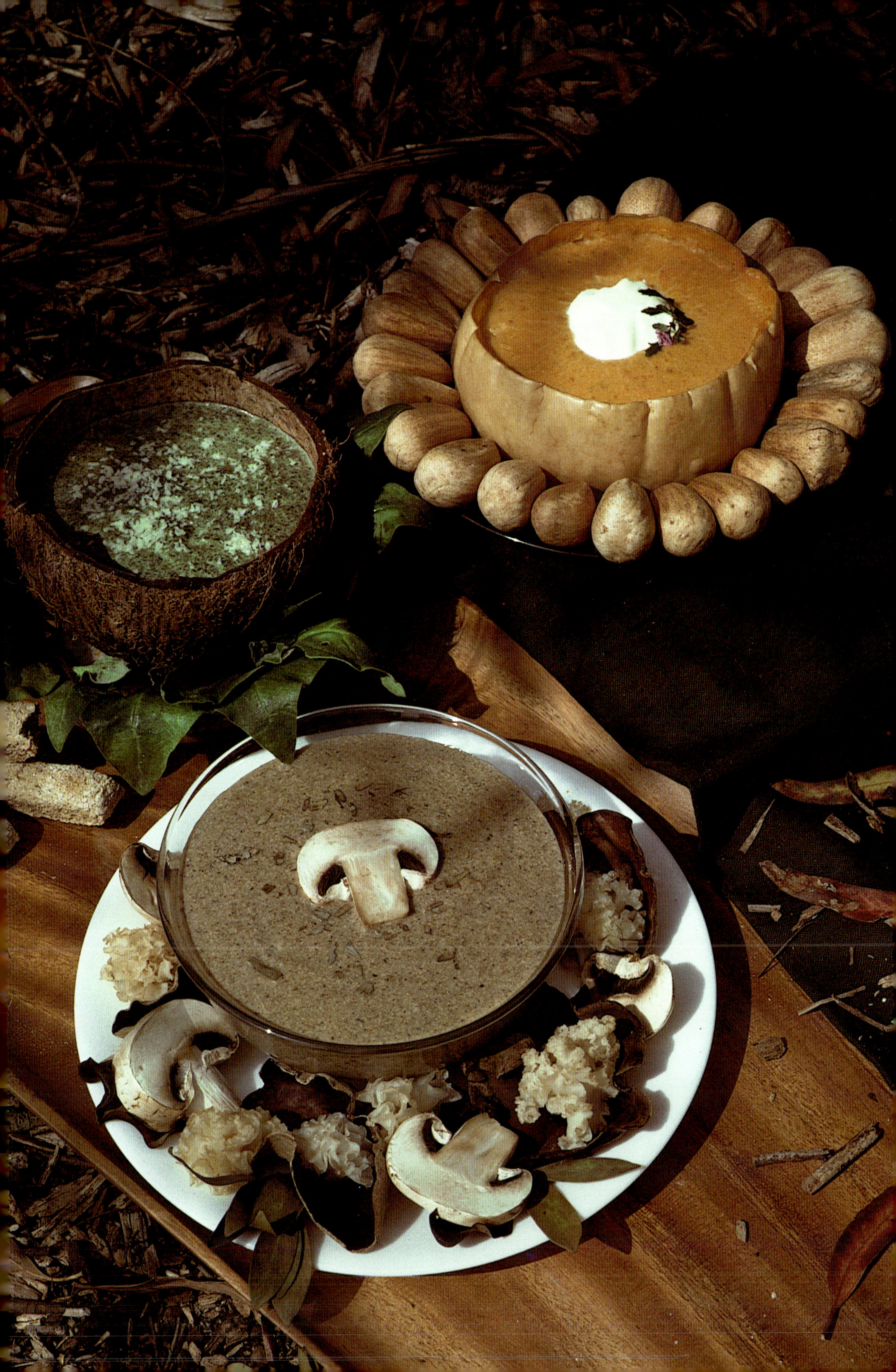

Roasted witjuti grubs

**4 witjuti grubs, frozen
1 teaspoon oil for frying**

Do not let the grubs thaw as they will go limp and blacken. Warm the oil in a skillet on medium heat and put in the frozen grubs. Turn the grubs often to stop them from leaking like sausages and losing their tasty contents. Fry the grubs until they are brown and crispy. Frozen grubs can also be roasted on a baking tray in a hot oven. Toss the grubs regularly.

Burrawang bread

**2 cups wholemeal flour
1 heaped tablespoon burrawang flour
1 teaspoon baking powder
½ teaspoon bread improver
water or milk**

Sift dry ingredients together twice. Adding water, knead into a dough and place it into a prepared bread tin. Dust the top with extra wholemeal flour and bake at 180°C for 30 minutes or until it sounds hollow when tapped. For the Bogong moth toasts recipe, once the loaf is cool, remove the crusts from several slices. Toast the slices then cut each into 2 or 3 fingers.

Eel spread

**1 cup chopped smoked eel
½ carton low-fat sour cream
1 cup wholemeal breadcrumbs**

Combine all ingredients in a food processor and blend to a smooth paste. Serve on bread fingers or biscuits

Bogong moth toasts

**a handful of Bogong moths
1 teaspoon macadamia oil
mozzarella cheese, grated
burrawang bread fingers**

In a mortar and pestle, mash the moths to a paste with the oil. Spread the paste onto burrawang bread fingers and and grill them. The spread can burn quickly so only grill long enough to heat the moth spread. Top with the grated cheese and place back under the griller to melt and brown the topping. Serve hot.

Witjuti grub dip

**5 large witjuti grubs
salt
½ carton low fat sour cream
125g ricotta cheese
1 teaspoon oil for frying**

Roast the grubs until well browned. Season them lightly then blend to a smooth paste with the remaining ingredients. Serve with burrawang bread pieces or wattle flatbread.

An alternative recipe uses the commercially available, canned Witchetty Grub Soup. To make the dip, reduce the contents of one can to a thick consistency and blend to a smooth paste with the sour cream and ricotta cheese as above.

From lower left: Roasted witjuti grubs, grub dip, moth toasts, smoked salmon, smoked roo with bush tomato chutney.
Rear plate: Eel spread on wattle flatbread, macadamia nuts.

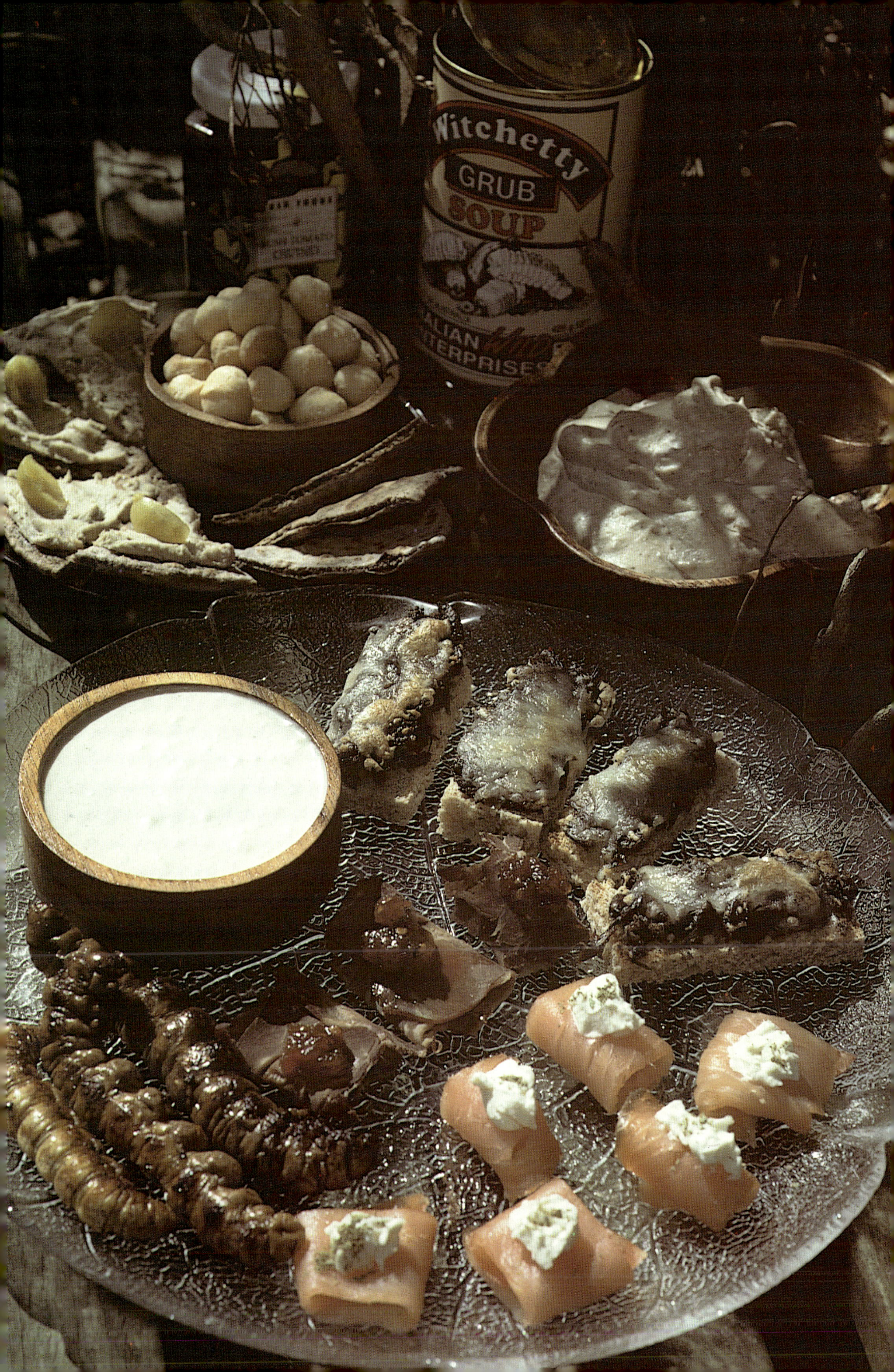
Witchetty
GRUB
SOUP

Smoked game, ratatouille and salad

smoked kangaroo or emu, sliced
bush tomato ratatouille
warrigal salad

Smoked meats can be sliced see-through thin by first freezing the meat and then machine slicing or using a very sharp knife.

Bush tomato ratatouille

1 tablespoon oil for frying
1 young eggplant, diced
1 large onion, chopped
½ cup bush tomatoes, ground
1 clove garlic, crushed
3 medium tomatoes, blanched, skinned and chopped
1 red capsicum, chopped
½ cup tomato sauce or ready-made spaghetti sauce
seasoning
a handful of whole bush tomatoes extra, (optional)

In oil, fry the eggplant until brown. Add the onion and garlic and sweat the onion until it is soft. Season with the ground bush tomatoes. Add the remaining ingredients and simmer until cooked. A few whole bush tomatoes can be added in the last 5 minutes. The ratatouille improves in flavour on refrigerated storage.

Warrigal salad

a handful of warrigal greens
native gooseberries
pear tomatoes
native violet flowers
macadamia oil
brown rice vinegar

Blanch warrigal greens in boiling water for 5 minutes and then transfer to ice cold water to retain the green colour. Drain. Toss with halved native gooseberry fruits, kangaroo apples and native violet flowers. Dress with macadamia oil and vinegar mixed in equal proportions.

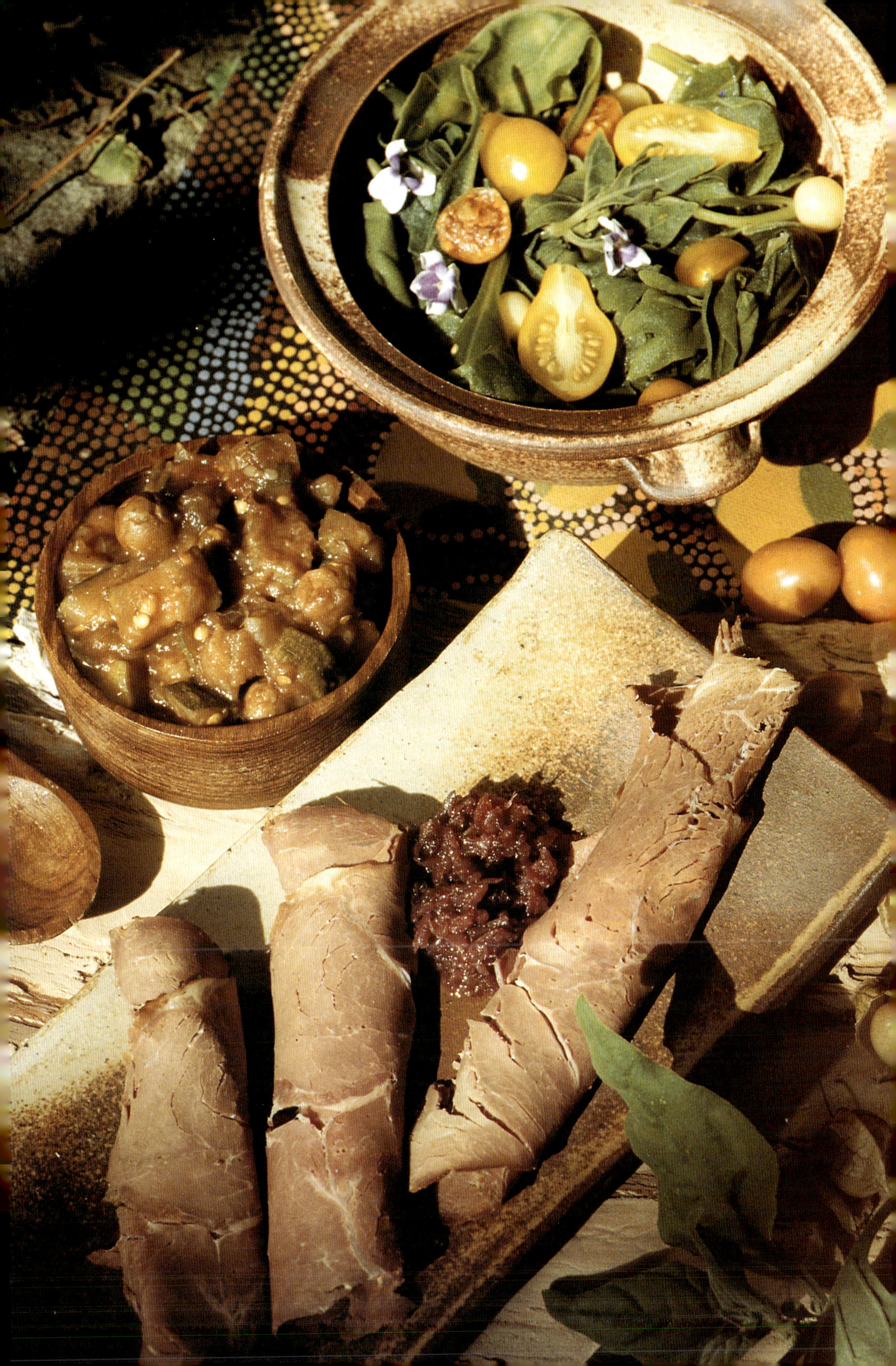

Uniquely Australian

Emu egg quiche

To serve 4

8 sheets prepared filo pastry
2 tablespoons butter, melted
1 emu egg or 7 chicken eggs
½ cup soy milk
seasoning
¾ cup water chestnuts, roasted and finely chopped
1 handful warrigal greens, blanched and finely chopped
½ cup ground bush tomatoes

Butter a quiche dish and layer the filo pastry in sheets, buttering each sheet. Cover the bottom and sides of the dish with pastry in this way and trim the edges. Beat the egg, soy milk and seasoning. Add the prepared chestnuts and warrigal greens and pour into the pastry case. Bake in a moderate oven for 40 minutes or until completely cooked. Sprinkle with the ground bush tomatoes before serving.

Grated cheese, sesame seeds and sunflower seeds can be added as additional toppings or add thinly sliced cassava, yams or kumara to the recipe.

Kangaroo quiche

To serve 4

2 cups brown rice, cooked with seaweed
butter
5 eggs
½ cup soy milk
¼ teaspoon salt
2 teaspoons finely ground native pepperleaf
1 onion, finely chopped and browned in butter
½ cup diced smoked kangaroo
2 teaspoons chopped native leek

The seaweed tends to make the rice sticky which makes a better quiche case. Use foraged kelp or the commercially available seaweed called kombu. Chop them finely and add to the rice as it cooks. Increase the volume of water a little as well (say, 2½ cups of water to 1 cup of rice). Butter a quiche dish and press the cooked rice in to form the crust. Beat together the eggs, soy milk, salt and half of the ground native pepperleaf. Spread the onion, kangaroo meat and chopped leeks over the prepared rice base, pour on the egg mixture and bake as above. Before serving, sieve the remaining ground pepperleaf over the quiche.

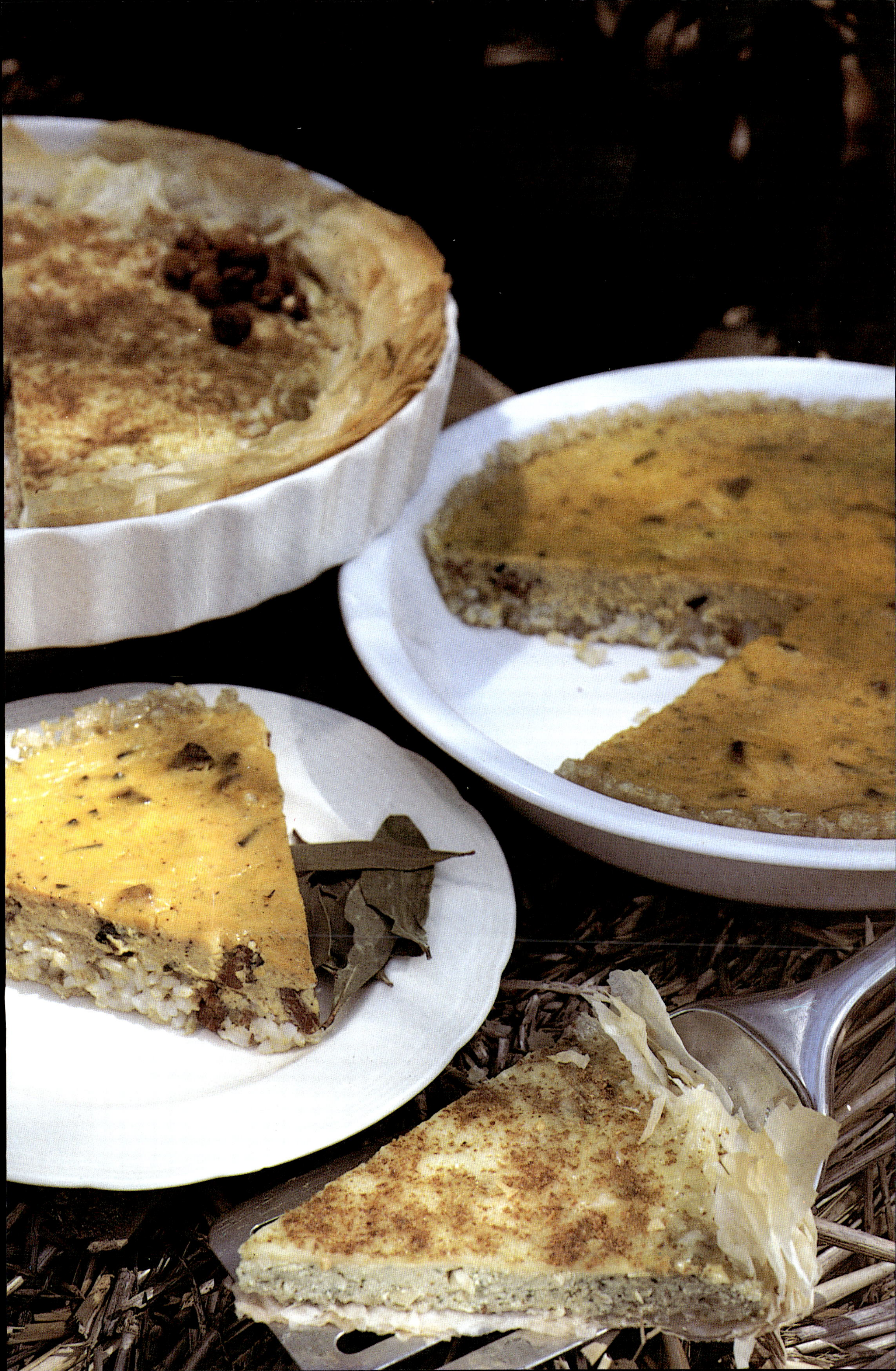

Filled vegetables make a convenient snack, finger food, side dish or main meal. If the vegetables can be cooked in a ground oven lined with paperbark the flavour from the bark can add to the other ingredients. Alternatively, individually wrap the vegetables in paperbark parcels and bake in a conventional oven before finishing them with your chosen filling.

Kumara boats 1.

kumara, halved and baked
water chestnuts, cooked, peeled and chopped finely
wild rice, cooked
soy milk
native pepper for seasoning

Scoop out kumara flesh leaving sufficient to keep the kumara boats firm. Fork together the kumara and chestnut mixture adding soy milk to moisten the mix. Season with native pepper. Fold in the wild rice and fill the kumara skins.

Kumara boats 2.

kumara, halved and baked
macadamia nuts, crushed

Scoop out the kumara flesh forming the boat. Fold the nuts through the mashed kumara and refill the boat.

Kumara or sweet potato is often called yam but is not even in the yam family. If native yams (Dioscorea species) are available they can be used as an alternative.

Stuffed tomatoes 1.

**tomatoes, halved and scooped
couscous
capsicum, finely chopped
kangaroo apples
native mint, finely chopped**

Mix the tomato seeds and pulp with the couscous and pour on boiling water as per the preparation instructions on the couscous package. Leave stand for 10 minutes until couscous softens. Push the kangaroo apples through a fine sieve and discard the seeds and skins. Combine the pulp with the remaining ingredients and fill the tomato halves. The stuffed tomatoes can be served cold or baked to soften the tomato halves.

Stuffed tomatoes 2.

**tomatoes, halved and scooped
ricotta cheese
rye bread crumbs
bush tomatoes, roughly chopped
black nightshade berries
seasoning**

Mix cheese, breadcrumbs and bush tomatoes. Season and then gently fold in the nightshade berries taking care not to squash too many of them.

Stuffed potatoes 1.

**baked potatoes, halved and scooped
bunya bunya nuts, boiled and shelled
seasoned wholemeal breadcrumbs
soy milk
native violet flowers**

In a blender combine 1 part bunya nuts, 2 parts potato and 1 part breadcrumbs. Add soy milk to make a firm paste. Fill the potato boats and garnish with violet flowers.

Stuffed potatoes 2.

**baked potatoes, halved and scooped
warrigal greens, blanched
ricotta cheese
native pepperleaf, ground**

Blend the potato, warrigal greens and ricotta until smooth. Season with the native pepper and refill the potato boats.

Stuffed potatoes 3.

**baked potatoes, halved and scooped
munthari fruits
macadamia nuts
mustard
native leeks for garnish**

Blend the macadamia nuts to smoothness. Add potato, munthari fruits and mustard to taste. Refill potato boats and garnish with the chopped native leek leaves.

Stuffed potatoes 4.

**baked potatoes, halved and scooped
refried kidney or navy beans
bush tomatoes, ground
grated cheese
native leeks for garnish**

Combine the potato, beans and bush tomato in a blender. Top with cheese, extra bush tomato sprinkle and garnish with the leeks.

Stuffed onions

**baked onions, topped and scooped
bush tomatoes, ground
butter for frying**

Chop the scooped onion and fry in butter. Once browned, season to taste with ground bush tomatoes. Refill the onion shells.

Polenta slice

To serve 8

1 cup coarse polenta (cornmeal)
3 cups water
½ cup butter
salt to taste
¼ teaspoon ground native pepperleaf
½ cup cheddar cheese, freshly grated (optional)
1 tablespoon butter
1 onion, finely diced
1 medium puffball or 6 pieces of Chinese white fungus
6 pieces shitake mushrooms, fresh or soaked
6 native morel mushrooms

In a saucepan, bring the water to the boil and slowly add the polenta in a thin stream while stirring constantly. Add the ½ cup of butter, salt and native pepper. Reduce the heat and simmer for 20 minutes or until the polenta is soft and thick. Stir frequently to stop the polenta from sticking. While the polenta is cooking, fry the onion in butter. Chop the mushrooms and cook them until tender then stir the mix into the cooked polenta. Add the cheddar cheese if desired. Pour the finished mix into a well-buttered glass dish and refrigerate until set.

This dish is more simply prepared in a microwave oven when it will not need to be stirred but still fry the onions and mushrooms to enhance their flavours.

Macadamia cheese sauce

1 cup macadamia nuts
soy milk
1 cup low-fat cheese, grated

Blend the macadamia nuts with a small amount of soy milk until smooth and creamy. Add the grated cheese and stir over a low heat to melt the cheese and thicken the sauce. Allow to cool and garnish with some chopped native leek leaves.

Pour over the polenta slice before serving and provide extra in a jug on the side. This sauce is bound to be popular. Try adding mustard or powdered native herbs and adding it to vegetable pies. The cheese can also be replaced with soy cream to make a dairy-free equivalent. Blended cooked bunya nuts can also be incorporated into the sauce to reduce the fat content by decreasing the amount of those high-fat macadamia nuts. Extra milk will be needed since bunya nuts absorb a great deal of liquid.

Uniquely Australian

This recipe is an interesting combination of two foods with similar histories. Corn was a traditional American Indian food and is now one of the eight world foods around which agriculture revolves. Macadamia has a much shorter history and less of an impact but it was a traditional food for east coast Australian Aborigines. It too has grown into a multi-million dollar crop moving from a rainforest forage staple into manufactured products including a gourmet oil, nut butter and a range of roasted packaged products.

Warrigal green roulade

To serve 8

500g warrigal greens, blanched, drained and chopped
3 red capsicums
10 eggs, separated
½ cup plain flour
½ bunch chives
500g cream cheese, softened
1 teaspoon ground native pepperleaf
seasoning

Roulade

Beat the egg yolks until creamy and then add sifted flour. Whip the egg whites. Add chopped warrigal greens to the yolk mixture. Season. Fold in whipped egg whites. Pour onto a baking paper lined tray. Spread evenly to a 2cm thickness and bake at 180°C for 15 minutes or until firm but not browned. Cool.

Filling

Wash and roast the red capsicums. Remove the skins and slice into strips. Chop the chives. Season the softened cream cheese with salt and the native pepper.

To assemble the roulade, turn the cooled roulade onto a piece of greaseproof paper or a tea towel and peel off the paper on which it was baked. If the paper does not come away easily spray water onto it and leave it a few minutes to dampen. It should now peel off. Spread the cream cheese evenly over the roulade and arrange the strips of capsicums and chives lengthwise. Roll up the roulade and chill it for 1 to 2 hours leaving it wrapped in greaseproof. Unwrap the greaseproof and slice the roulade.

Uniquely Australian

The warrigal greens can also be supplemented or replaced with blanched portulaca stems. Portulaca has been shown to contain a significant concentration of the particular polyunsaturated oils recommended by nutritionists for their protective role against heart disease.

Kurrajong and spice focaccia

1kg sourdough (see below)
100g finely ground kurrajong flour
2 teaspoons ground native pepperleaf
1 tablespoon ground native aniseed leaf
or lemon myrtle leaf
4 large onions, finely chopped
2 tablespoons ground bush tomatoes
½ teaspoon sea salt
macadamia oil
wild fennel seeds

Thoroughly mix all ingredients except oil and fennel seeds into the dough and proof for ½ hour. Divide into 250g rounds then flatten to about 2cm. Dimple the top with your fingers and brush lavishly with macadamia nut oil. Sprinkle wild fennel seeds on top. Proof on a tray for 1 hour, then bake at 180°C for 20-25 minutes. Store leftover focaccia bread in plastic bags (not freezer bags) and frozen for use as required.

Wattle and bunya focaccia

1kg sourdough
100g spent wattle seed
200g bunya nuts
500g onions, finely chopped
1 teaspoon sea salt
macadamia oil
sesame seeds

Boil, shell and chop the bunya nuts. Allow to cool and then follow the recipe as for the kurrajong and spice focaccia.

Making your own sourdough

⅔ cups wholemeal flour
1 cup filtered water
a pinch of salt

Chlorinated or sulphated water will rarely produce a good sourdough. Use filtered water to mix with the sifted flour and salt to produce a medium consistency batter. Add the water slowly while mixing well to avoid any lumps. Place in a glass or earthenware bowl, cover with a cotton cloth and leave at room temperature for 2 to 5 days until bubbles appear showing that the batter is obviously active. Mix the sourdough starter with the same quantity of flour and water and allow it to ferment again. The leaven is now ready to use. To produce a sourdough, stir the leaven and then mix 1 cup of leaven with 3 cups of flour. Add filtered water and a little salt to make a soft stretchy dough. Mix the remaining cupful of leaven with more flour and water back to the batter consistency. Store in a jar and keep refrigerated. When required for use, it can be left for an hour or so to warm up and then mixed into a dough.

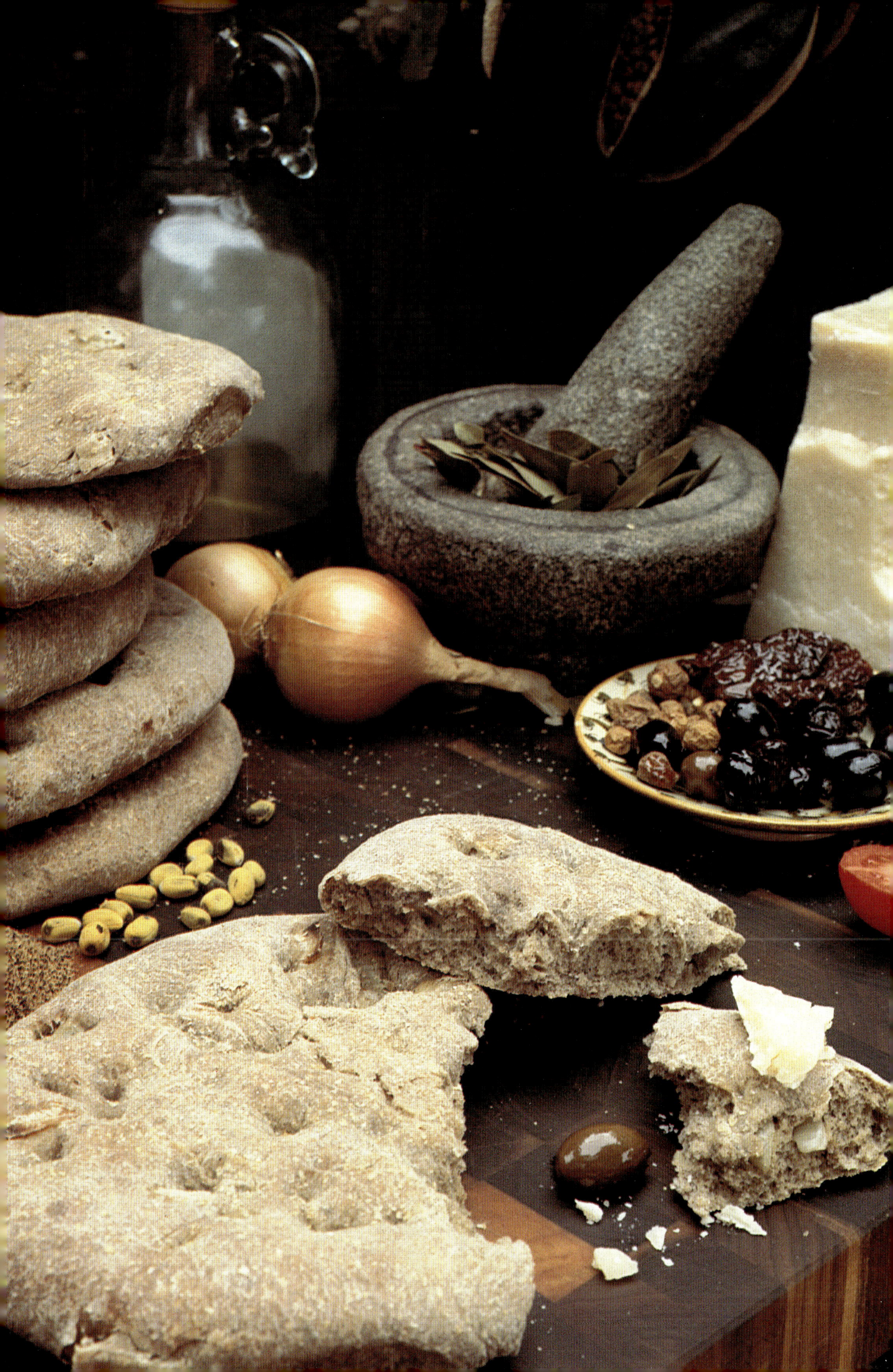

Pasta

Basic pasta recipe

250g plain flour
150g semolina flour
4 medium eggs
¼ teaspoon salt
water, if necessary

To the basic recipe add either:

2 large handfuls of warrigal greens, blanched, well squeezed and chopped

or **½ cup wattle**

or **⅔ cup ground bush tomatoes**

or **¼ cup burrawang flour**

In a food processor, mix the dry ingredients then add the eggs one at a time and if making the warrigal pasta add the warrigal greens with the eggs. Water may need to be added for the mixture to form a stiff dough which should ball in the food processor. Remove the dough from the processor bowl and knead by hand for 3 to 5 minutes. Cover the dough with a tea towel and leave to rest for 30 minutes. Pass the rested dough through a pasta machine until the desired thickness is achieved. Cook as for fresh pasta.

Other pasta can be made using kurrajong flour, bunya nut meal, native pepper, lemon myrtle or macadamia nut meal. Sauces, if any, should be simple and flavours chosen to complement the delicate pastas.

Try cooking wattle pasta in wattle. Boil a
heaped tablespoon of wattle in a litre of
water. Strain the wattle reserving the liquid.
Use this to cook the wattle pasta.

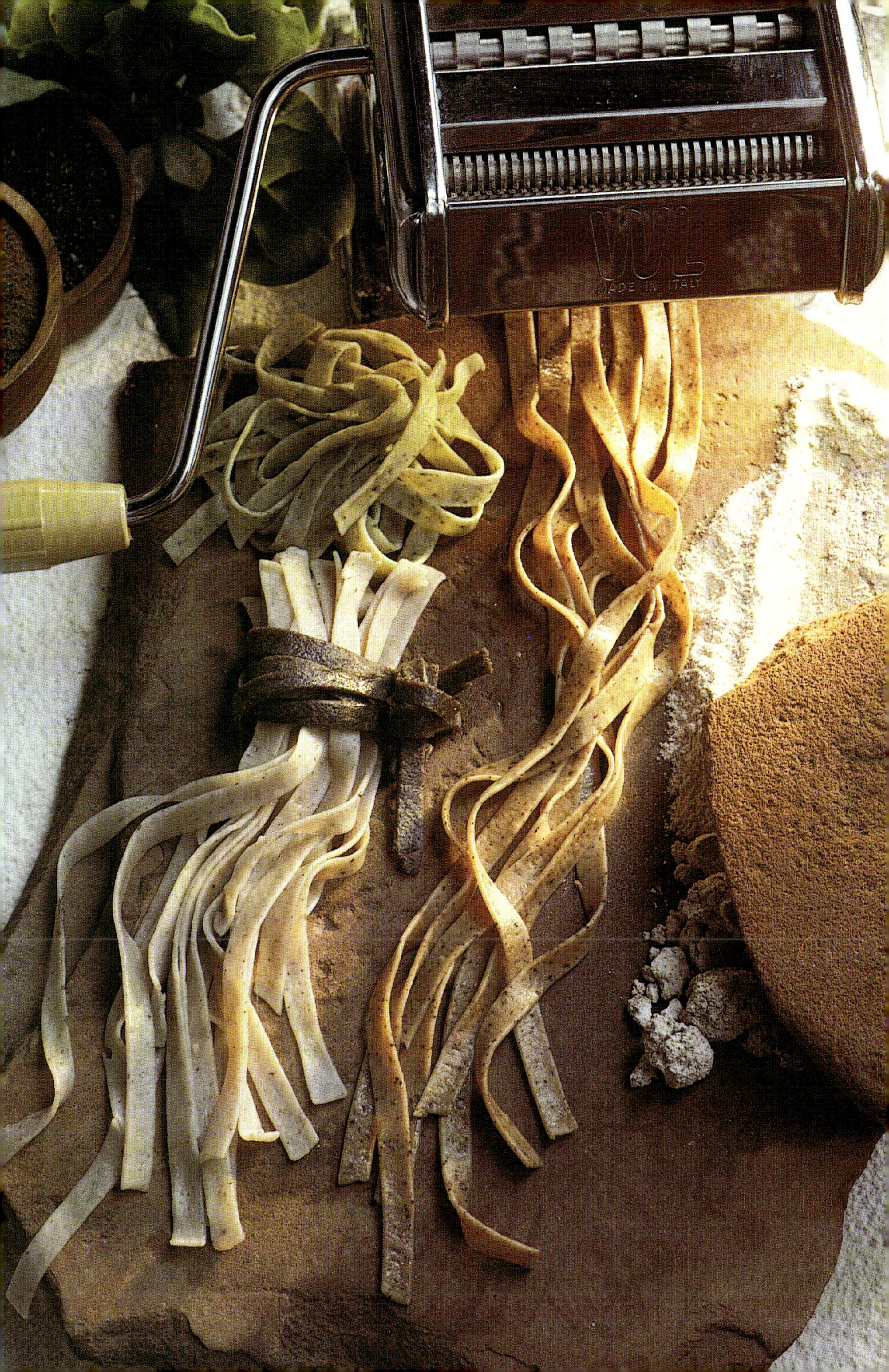
MADE IN ITALY

Yabby ravioli

Pasta

3 eggs
1 tablespoon oil
250g plain flour

Lightly beat the eggs and add the oil. Place the flour into a food processor bowl and slowly add the egg mixture while processing to form a dough. Remove the dough, wrap it with a tea towel and let it rest in the refrigerator for 1 hour.

Yabby filling

12 to 15 yabbies, cooked and shelled
1 onion, diced
1 tablespoon butter
2 eggs
salt
pepper
juice from 1 lemon
⅓ cup cream

Blend the yabby tails in a food processor. Fry the onion in butter and add to the yabby meat. Add the remaining ingredients and blend to a smooth paste. Chill.

Ravioli

Roll out the pasta to 2mm thickness and cut out rounds 8cm in diameter. Brush half way around the edge with milk or a beaten egg Place yabby filling in the centre of each round. Fold over to form a semi-circle and crimp the edge with a fork. Drop the ravioli into a large volume of boiling salted water and cook for 6 to 8 minutes until tender.
Drain and sprinkle with macadamia oil.

Alternatively, serve the ravioli with a light cream sauce flavoured with lemon aspen juice and native pepper leaves or use burrawang flour in the pasta mix.

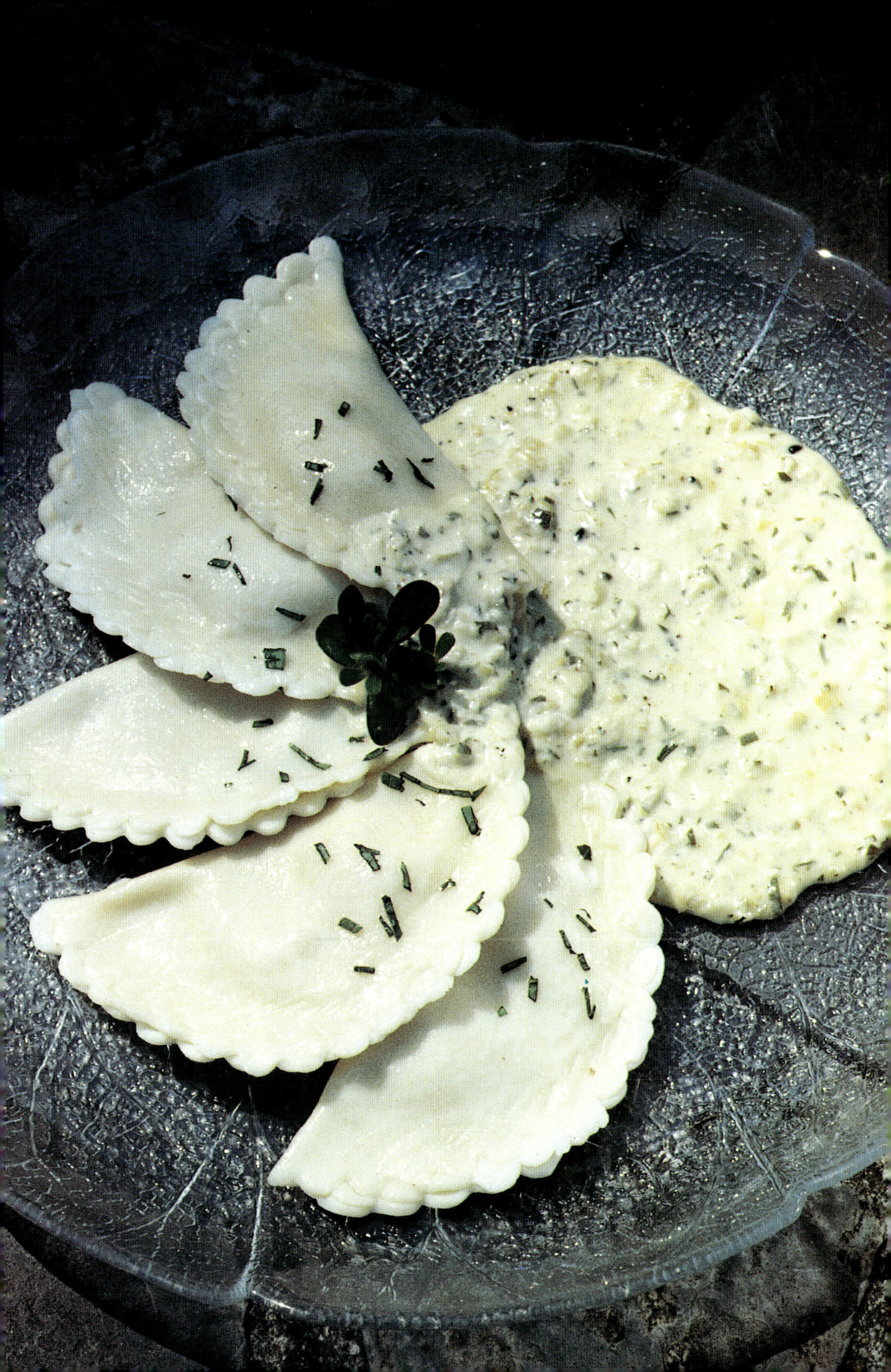

Wild spaghetti sauces

To serve 2

Illawarra plum and bush tomato

1 cup Illawarra plums
½ cup bush tomatoes
onion
2 medium tomatoes, one skinned

Blend the Illawarra plums, bush tomatoes, fried onion and the skinned tomato to smoothness. Season to taste. Chop the remaining tomato and stir into the mixture. Serve over warrigal pasta.

Macadamia nut and warrigal greens

1 handful warrigal greens, blanched
50g macadamia nuts, raw or roasted
2 small onions, chopped
4 large mushrooms, sliced
3 tablespoons sour cream
macadamia nut oil for frying
seasonings

Finely chop the warrigal greens and less finely, chop the macadamia nuts. Gently fry the onions in macadamia nut oil and just sweat the mushrooms briefly. Combine all the ingredients and toss to coat the warrigal greens with the sour cream. Serve over burrawang pasta.

Native mint salad

10 sugar peas
½ cup mung seeds
½ cup English garden peas
1 small sprig native mint
2 tablespoons macadamia nut oil
native leeks, chopped

Briefly steam or microwave the peas and mung seeds with the mint. Toss with the macadamia nut oil. Garnish with the leeks and serve over a bush tomato pasta.

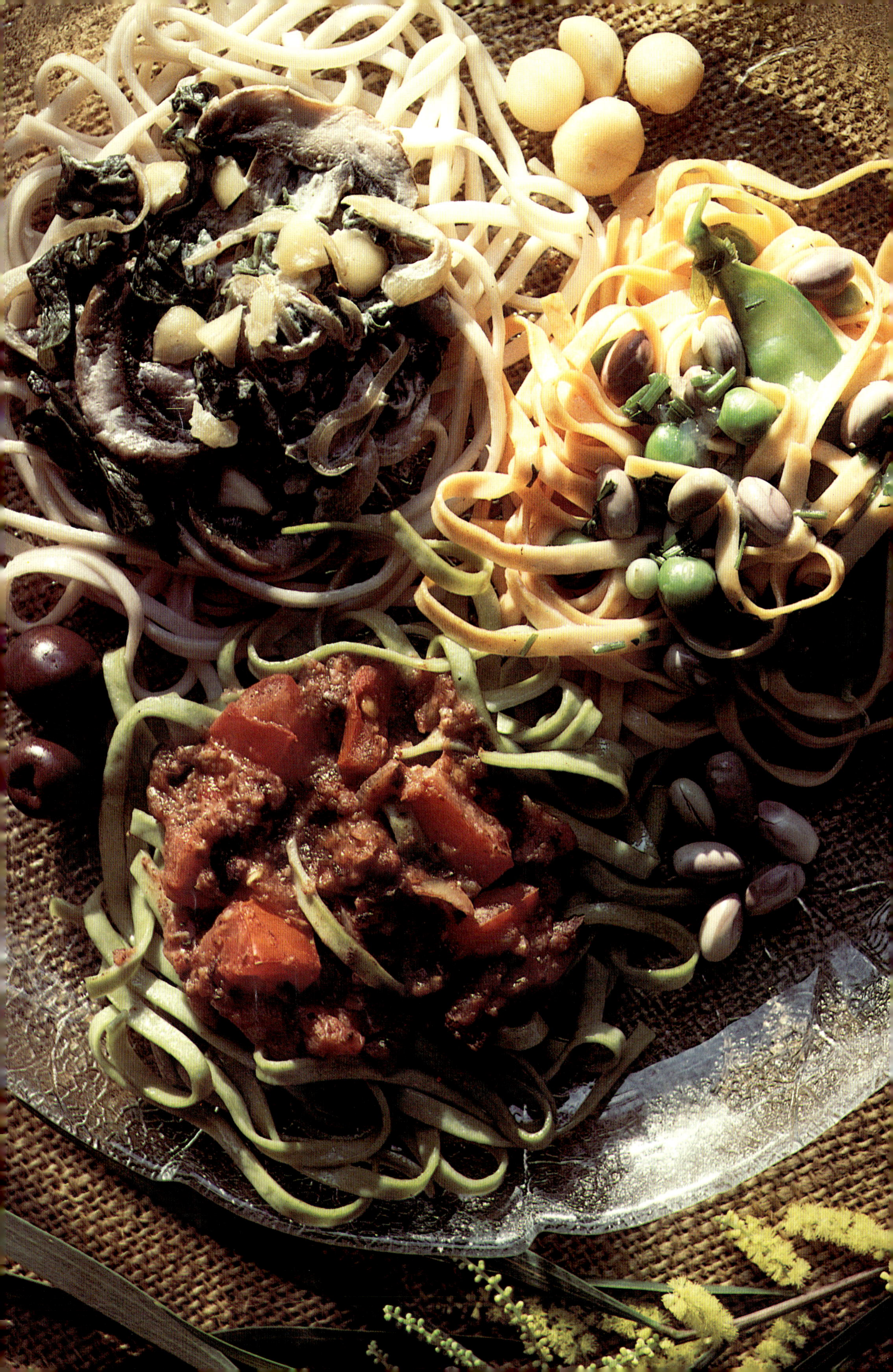

Sausages and burgers

These recipes are suitable for either filling into sausage skins or simply frying as burgers. Sausages may benefit from the addition of fat, preferably goose fat, to make them more juicy. Naturally this makes them higher in energy and so they should not be eaten as often or alternatively, work a little harder to burn up the kilojoules when chasing the primary ingredients.

Kangaroo or emu burgers

1 kg kangaroo backstrap or emu saddle
2 teaspoons cracked black pepper
1 teaspoon freshly ground native pepperleaf
1 teaspoon salt
1 small onion, chopped and fried
½ clove garlic, crushed and fried
1 chicken egg

Crocodile and wattle burgers

1 kg crocodile meat
3 tablespoons wattle boiled in ½ cup water
½ teaspoon green or pink peppercorns
1 teaspoon salt
1 chicken egg

Buffalo and native mint burgers

1 kg buffalo tenderloin
3 sprigs of native mint (about ¼ cup of very loosely packed leaves)
1 teaspoon cracked black pepper
1 teaspoon salt
½ teaspoon ground nutmeg
1 small onion, chopped and fried
1 chicken egg

The red meats can be marinated in about 500ml of red wine for added richness of flavour. Coarsely mince the meat and mix in the remaining ingredients adding the egg to bind the mixture. Extra seasoning can be added to taste. Pan fry in macadamia nut oil and serve with fried onions seasoned with akudjura (ground bush tomatoes).

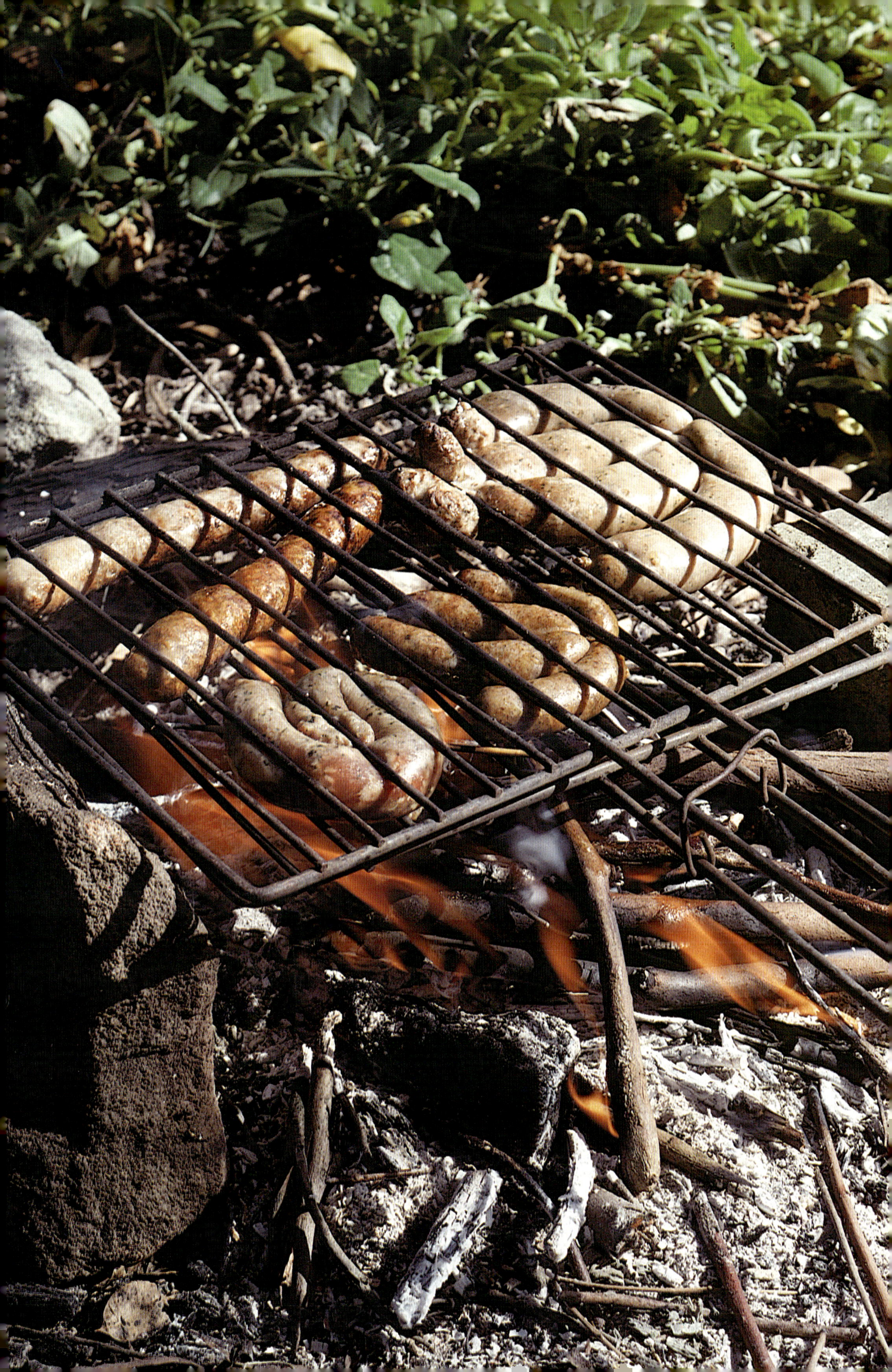

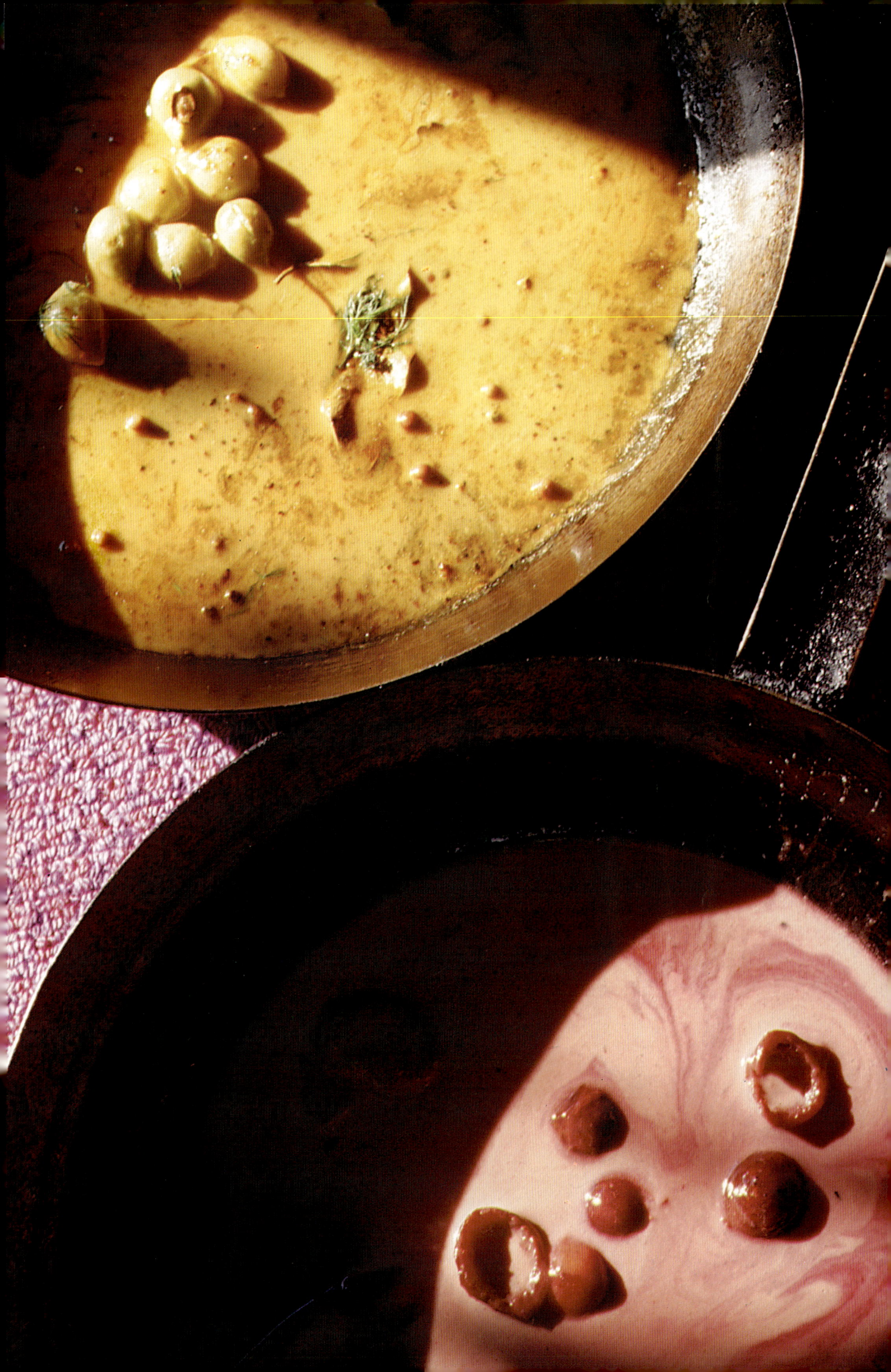

Fine dining

The following recipes give some insight into the many and varied ways to use the commercially available bushfoods. The recipes include those contributed by chefs, cooks and other professionals in the food service industry. Among the recipes, there are some which reflect our British colonial past. Other offerings follow foreign traditions, some are as uniquely Australian as emus and kangaroos and some present dishes which are characteristic of particular geographic regions.

Each of the recipes could be described as food-art made from styled, colourful dishes set for service. They were all tempting and delicious. Most of the recipes are elegant in their simplicity because they were designed for restaurant service. This makes them very practical for preparation at home. In addition, the intention of each of the meals is to inspire as well as to provide ideas on food combination and presentation. A quick pre-dinner flick through any well-photographed cookery book refines our preferences for the planned meal ahead and stimulates our own culinary creativity. This is modified by the ingredients at hand and it becomes easy to substitute, improvise, modify and style our own pièce de résistance. We eat for hedonistic reasons as well as for sustenance, the organoleptic qualities of foods; how they stimulate the senses, prepares us for the cooking as well as the dining experience. Anticipation is often as enjoyable as participation. The actual ingredients are often less important and are meant to be changed. Make a dish conform to your own taste by altering the quantities of flavourings or changing them altogether. One aim is never to make the same dish twice. There are so many possibilities, why limit yourself?

Uniquely Australian

Soused Coorong mullet with munthari

To serve 1

250g Coorong mullet fillets, trimmed
300ml cider vinegar
½ cup brown sugar (optional)
1 chilli, chopped
25g munthari
seasonings
several sprigs of coriander
finely sliced vegetables for garnish

Simmer the vinegar, sugar and chilli for 5 to 10 minutes. Take off the boil and pour over the fish and munthari. Leave for 3 or 4 minutes until the fillets are cooked through. Plate up the fish and munthari and serve at once or refrigerate the fillets in the vinegar and serve cold. Garnish with coriander and a colourful mix of vegetables. Try this recipe with a native herb vinegar or a pre-prepared munthari vinegar.

Aborigines of the Sydney region also fished for mullet and used the Sydney golden wattle, Acacia longifolia, as a calendar plant: When it flowered Aborigines knew to move towards the coast. The plants were telling the locals that the mullet were ready to hunt. The fish could be found in large schools just off-shore and were at the peak of their life cycle.

This recipe is parochially South Australian with the two principle ingredients from in and around the Coorong district in the south of the State. The method is an easy way to cook fish in a billy out bush and fragrant leaves or any local wild fruits can be used.

70

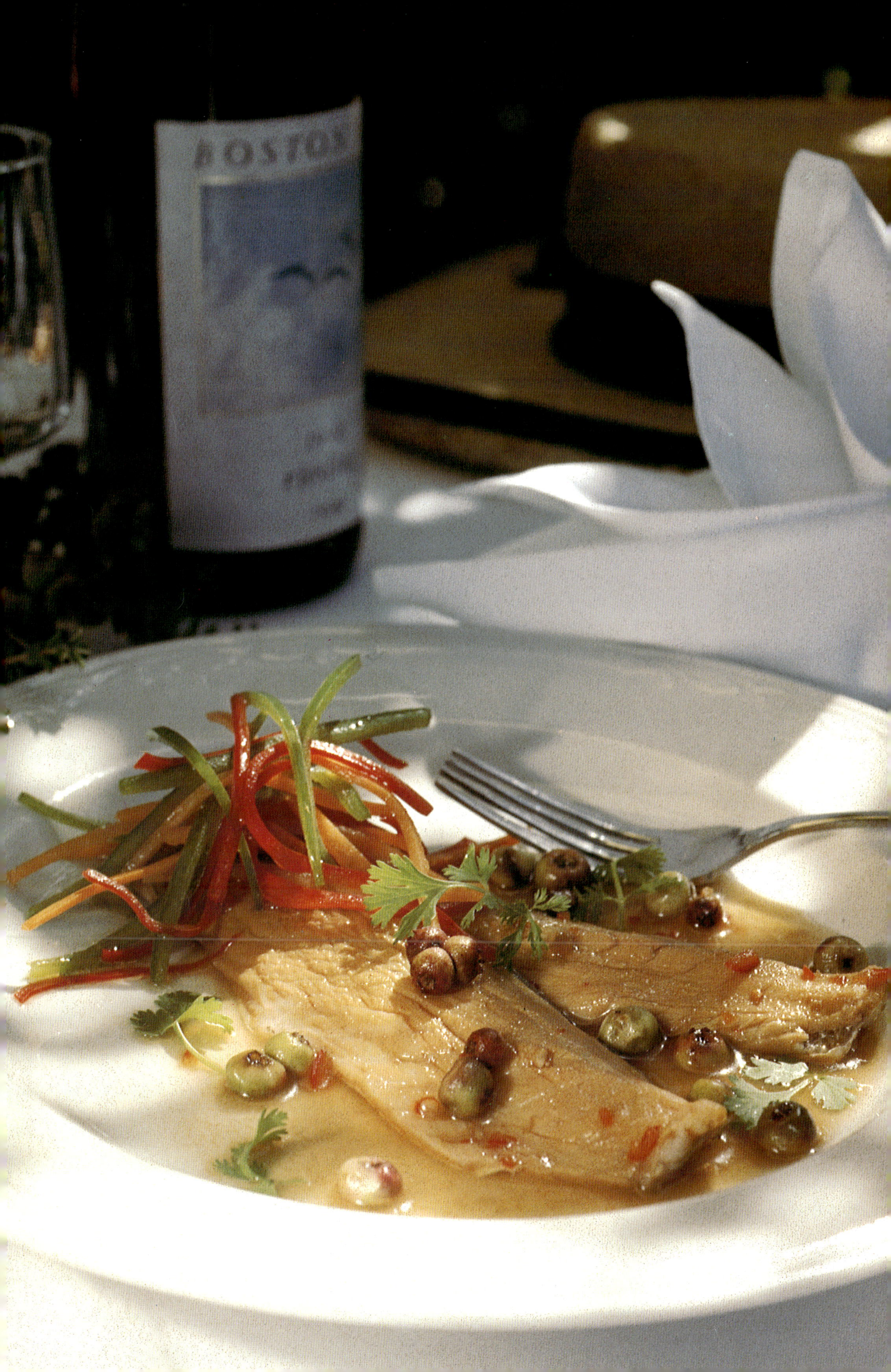

Moreton Bay bugs on kurrajong pancakes

To serve 4

20 Moreton Bay bugs
kurrajong pancakes
lemon aspen mayonnaise

Pancakes

1 cup self raising flour
1 egg
30g kurrajong flour
50ml milk
pinch salt
butter or oil for frying

Mix the batter and immediately prepare 4 pancakes. If the batter is left to stand the oils in the kurrajong flour tend to split the mix.

Lemon aspen mayonnaise

50g lemon aspen fruits, juiced
3 egg yolks
1 teaspoon French mustard
150ml white wine vinegar
500ml macadamia oil
seasonings

Blend the ingredients in a food processor.

Remove the shells from the bugs by cutting and removing the side spikes along the edge of the tail and peeling away the shell in halves. Poach the tails in boiling salted water for 1½ to 2 minutes.

To serve, arrange the tails on the prepared pancakes and serve them dressed with the lemon aspen mayonnaise.

Uniquely Australian

Moreton Bay bugs or bay lobsters are found around Australia's northern coast from the North West Cape in Western Australia to Moreton Bay near Brisbane, Queensland. Balmain bugs or shovel nosed sand lobsters are the south-eastern equivalent although the two crustaceans are not closely related. Balmain bugs have their eyes in the centre of their heads while Moreton Bay lobsters have their eyes on the outer edge of their heads.

It is interesting that the marine bugs and other species of crayfish and lobsters are regarded as culinary delicacies while insects such as witjuti grubs and Bogong moths suffer from a cultural cringe. This is all the more interesting when grubs survive on sugars and a little wood pulp and the moths are nectar feeders whereas the marine animals are scavengers eating whatever they can find alive, dead or decaying on the ocean floor.

The size of Balmain bugs and of many species of seafood has been falling noticeably over the last fifteen years. Over-fishing a limited resource, allowing ever smaller animals to be taken to satisfy a growing demand may stop as fish farming becomes more economically attractive but another cause of size reduction, particularly in molluscs, may be pollution. The Sydney mud oyster, once common along the waterways of the Parramatta and Lane Cove Rivers even up until the second World War were an important food for Aborigines. The dinner-plate sized oysters are now either locally extinct or rarely found much larger than a chicken's egg.

The farmed yabby could be substituted for the bugs in this recipe if desired.

Sardines in macadamia nut oil

To serve 4

20 sardines
500ml water
50g sea salt
300ml macadamia nut oil
1 lemon or 5 lemon aspen fruits, juiced
1 oak leaved lettuce
pickled Illawarra plums
pickled Kakadu plums

Clean, gut and wash the sardines. Make up a 10% salt solution of the salt in water. Pickle the fish in the salt solution for 6 to 8 hours. Remove the sardines and wash them in fresh water. Drain. Bring 4 litres of water to the boil and gently poach the sardines in the simmering water for 1½ to 2 minutes. Drain and cool.
Transfer to a marinade made from macadamia nut oil and the lemon or lemon aspen juice. Leave to marinate for between four hours and four days in the refrigerator.

To serve, lay out the sardines onto absorbent paper to remove any excess marinade. Arrange five fish per plate onto the oak lettuce leaves and serve with steamed asparagus and a combination of pickled Illawarra and Kakadu plums.

Pickled native plums

Illawarra or Kakadu plums
lemon myrtle vinegar
native aniseed vinegar

Bring the vinegars to the boil in separate saucepans. Pour each onto either of the plums packed in sterile jars. Seal and store in a cool pantry or cupboard for at least a month. Do not boil the plums or their skins will break. For a quicker pickling (about a week or so), prick the skins of the plums to allow the vinegar to penetrate better.

Uniquely Australian

This recipe contrasts the oily fish and marinade with the acid pickle of the plums.

Yabbies and whiting with lemon aspen butter sauce

To serve 1

3 yabbies
1 large whiting fillet
6-8 young samphire shoots
lemon aspen butter sauce

If the yabbies are live, place them in a freezer for 30 minutes and then boil them briefly in salted water flavoured with a few crushed lemon aspen fruits. Refresh in iced water and peel the tails and claws, reserving one yabby whole for garnish. Arrange the whiting fillet in a cone shape on a steamer tray with the yabby tails, body and samphire. Steam for 3 to 4 minutes. Serve at once with lemon aspen butter sauce.

Lemon aspen butter sauce

50g lemon aspen, chopped
50ml lemon juice
150ml fish stock
100ml white wine
250g unsalted butter, diced

Simmer the fruit and liquids until reduced to a syrup consistency. Gently swirl in the butter, a few pieces at a time until it is all incorporated. Season to taste and pass the sauce through a fine sieve.

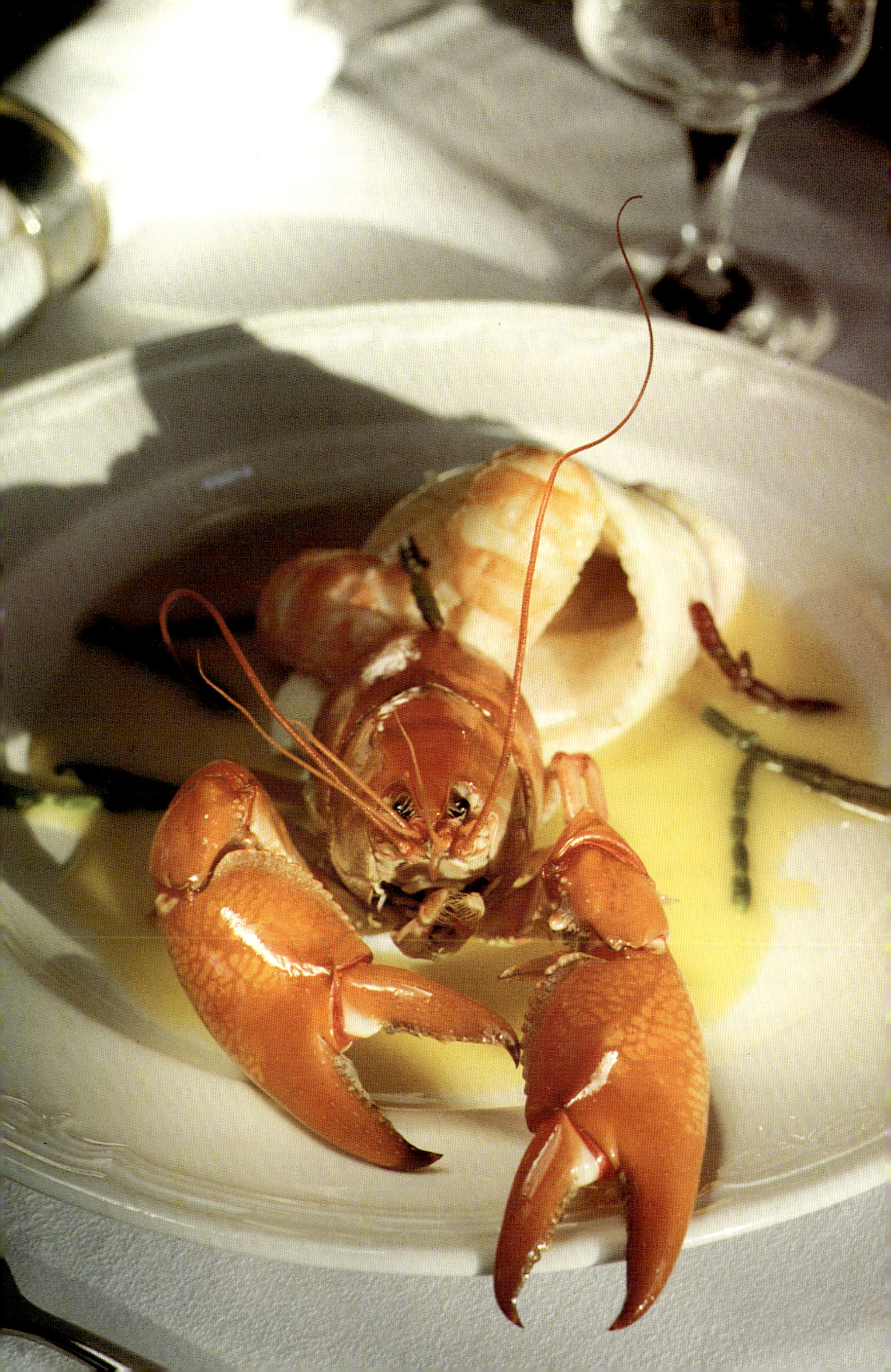

Moreton Bay bugs 'Eumundi'

To serve 2

Beer batter

1 tablespoon wattle
8 chopped chives
150g plain flour
100g corn flour
350ml Eumundi beer
oil or butter for frying

Bring the wattle to the boil in a small amount of the beer. Cool. Combine the dry ingredients and mix to a smooth batter with the wattle beer and the remainder of the beer. Leave to stand for 30 minutes and then adjust the consistency if necessary.

4 large bugs
plain flour for dusting
1 litre macadamia nut oil

Using kitchen scissors, cut the spined edges from the tails and remove the shells. Coat the meat in flour and dip into the batter. Place them into hot but not smoking oil and cook for 3 to 4 minutes, turning every 30 seconds or so. Remove and drain on absorbent paper.

Serve the tails with salad and a relish.

The remaining batter can be made into savoury pancakes.
Add a pinch of salt and a teaspoon of baking powder and
fry the pancakes or try adding just the pinch of salt and
leaving the batter to sour for two days.

Uniquely Australian

Eumundi beer and Moreton Bay bugs are both native to the Sunshine State of Queensland.

Uniquely Australian

Barramundi with muntharies

To serve 1

**30ml vegetable oil
2 drops edible eucalyptus oil
400g barramundi, filleted
1 tablespoon butter
30g leek, cut to diamonds
1 lemon myrtle leaf
½ cup muntharies
seasonings**

Combine the vegetable oil and the eucalyptus oil and heat in a frypan to smoking temperature. Pan fry the fillets until the skin is crispy (about 2 minutes). Turn the fillets over and cook the other side (1 minute or less). Set aside in a warm dish. In the same pan, melt the butter then add the leek, lemon myrtle and muntharies and toss until cooked.
Season and serve over the fillets.

If the barramundi is whole, reserve the entrails to prepare fish fries (see page 32). Chopped fish fries can be served as an accompaniment to this dish or made into a sauce as
an alternative flavouring.

Uniquely Australian

This is a good recipe for substitution with whatever seafood and bush fruits are available.

Marron with macadamia nut and native lime mayonnaise

To serve 2

6 live marron
1 onion, carrot and celery stalk
1 teaspoon whole peppercorns
white wine
water

Place the marron into the freezer for 10 minutes and then into rapidly boiling, salted water with onion, carrot, celery, peppercorns and a good slurp of white wine. Simmer for only 1½ to 2 minutes. Overcooking will destroy the delicate flavour. Remove the cooked marron from the water and dip briefly into iced water. Arrange 3 per plate.

Serve with fresh fruits, green salad and the macadamia nut and native lime mayonnaise.

Native lime mayonnaise

25g roasted macadamia nuts
5 native limes
3 egg yolks
2 tablespoons white wine vinegar
1 teaspoon seeded mustard
500ml macadamia nut oil

Combine the mayonnaise ingredients and blend to smoothness.

Uniquely Australian

Any crustacean can be used including saltwater species.

Prawns on a wattle pancake

To serve 4

20 green prawns, seasoned
50ml native lime juice
250ml fish stock
100ml cream
60g butter
12 leaves warrigal greens
assorted vegetable batons, blanched
2 tablespoons macadamia nut oil

Pan fry the seasoned prawns in half the macadamia oil and set aside. Add the native lime juice and fish stock to the pan and reduce the volume by half. Add the cream and allow the sauce to simmer for 2 minutes. Remove from the heat and melt in the cold butter. In a separate pan, heat the remaining macadamia oil, fry off the warrigal greens and vegetable batons.

Wattle pancakes

1 egg
1 cup self raising flour seasoned with
paprika, pepper and mixed herbs
1 tablespoon boiled wattle
50ml milk
salt
butter or oil for frying

Mix all the ingredients into a batter and leave to stand for 30 minutes. Fry 4 pancakes using a small egg ring.

To serve, pour some of the sauce onto each plate, arrange 3 leaves of warrigal greens per plate, place the wattle pancake, lay out the prawns and garnish with the vegetable batons.

Uniquely Australian

Wattle pancakes can be either savoury or sweet and can be garnished with a wide range of accompaniments.

Uniquely Australian

Trim the fins and tail of the gutted trout.

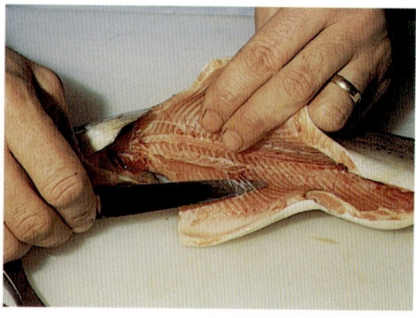

With a sharp knife, cut the ribs from the muscle wall.

Firmly holding the head, cut down both sides of the backbone.

Lay out the trout and remove the backbone.

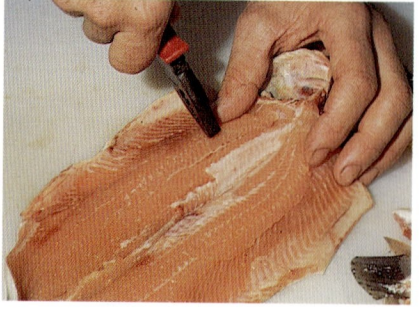

Feel for bones and remove them using a pair of pliers or forceps.

Use fillets of fish, shellfish or molluscs as filling. Fruits can also be included.

Arrange the seafood and fruits as stuffing.

Place the filled trout and a sprig of lemon scented tea tree onto the paperbark.

Tie the paperbark with string or vine and steam in boiling water with vegetables or bake in the oven.

Uniquely Australian

Rainbow trout and seafood

To serve 2

**1 rainbow trout, boned out
2 sprigs of lemon tea tree
1 sheet of paperbark to wrap trout
4 prawns
8 scallops
2 red emperor fillets
3 small octopus
6 lemon aspen fruits, juiced**

Place the boned trout with a sprig of tea tree on the paperbark. Fill the cavity of the trout with seafood mix and pour on the lemon aspen juice. Cover the stuffed trout with the remaining tea tree then wrap and tie the paperbark parcel with string. Place the prepared fish into a tray with pre-heated salted water and a few vegetables and bake at 275°C for about 30 minutes.

Sauce

**½ can Witchetty Grub Soup™
6 native aniseed leaves
1 handful warrigal greens, blanched**

To make the sauce, add the aniseed leaves to the half can of soup and reduce the volume to thicken the consistency. Cream can be added if desired. Add the chopped warrigal greens.

To serve, unwrap the paperbark at the table and serve with extra warrigal greens and the Witchetty Grub Soup™ sauce. If the soup is unavailable use whole grubs to make a stock.

Uniquely Australian

Chargrilled crocodile

To serve 2

2 x 100g crocodile steaks
fresh ginger
garlic
fresh peppercorns
2 teaspoons macadamia oil
150g bunya nuts, boiled and shelled
3 teaspoons wattle
50ml chicken stock
50ml dry white wine
100ml cream
chives for garnish

Marinate the crocodile steaks overnight with the ginger, garlic and peppercorns. Cook the crocodile on a char-grill over tea tree branches. Turn 2 or 3 times only to cook to medium rare.

In a hot pan, lightly fry the bunya nuts in the oil. When browned, add the wattle, the stock, wine and cream and reduce to thicken.

Serve the sauce over the crocodile and garnish with the chopped chives.

Uniquely Australian

Wattle complements the delicate (almost bland) flavour of crocodile making wattle crocodile an Australian alternative to the Thai style, coffee chicken.

Not all Aboriginal groups in northern Australia used the salt water crocodile as food. Those who did, hunted the smaller animals and prized the tail for its fat and flavour. Even the backbone was pounded and eaten supplying valuable minerals, particularly calcium and phosphorus. Both of these were important for Aborigines whose diet was traditionally dairy-free. Desert Aborigines also processed lizards in a similar fashion. Undoubtedly, the marrow improved the flavour of the meat due to its high content of fats.

Uniquely Australian

Bunya nut vegetarian pie

To serve 10 to 12

Pastry

butter for frying
1 small onion, chopped
2 teaspoons of rosemary
⅓ cup of cream
250g bunya bunya nuts

In a large frying pan, melt the butter and fry the onion with the rosemary until soft but not brown. Finely mince the bunya nuts to a meal and add this to the rosemary onions. Add the fresh cream. Cook while stirring until the mixture gets to the consistency of pastry. Cool for 5 minutes then press into an unbuttered, loose-bottomed pie plate.

Filling

2 large tomatoes
2 handfuls warrigal greens
2 large broccoli heads
1 medium kumara, thinly sliced
4 large mushrooms, sliced
Chinese five spices
carrot, grated
ground coriander seeds
1 large onion
1 clove garlic
a pinch of cumin
red capsicum, chopped
fenugreek seeds, ground

butter
corn or macadamia nut oil
½ cup cream
200g mature cheddar cheese, grated
seasoning

The same volume of boiling water can be used to cook the bunya nuts and blanch the tomatoes and warrigal greens. The broccoli and kumara slices can also be lightly steamed at the same time. In sequence in a frying pan, stir-fry the mushrooms in butter with a little Chinese five spice. Then fry the grated carrot in corn oil with ground coriander seeds. Next sweat the onions and garlic in corn oil with a pinch of cumin and finally fry the capsicum in corn oil. Prepare the topping in the same pan by reducing by half the cream with the broccoli and fenugreek. Top with the grated cheese and put the pan under the grill to melt the cheese over the broccoli. Put aside to cool. Assemble the pie by layering the onions, kumara, carrot, warrigal greens and mushroom. Place the broccoli and cheese top and finish with the capsicum and sliced tomato.
Cover the pie with greased foil so that the foil stands proud of the cheese topping and bake for 1 hour at 250°C. Cool a little before slicing.

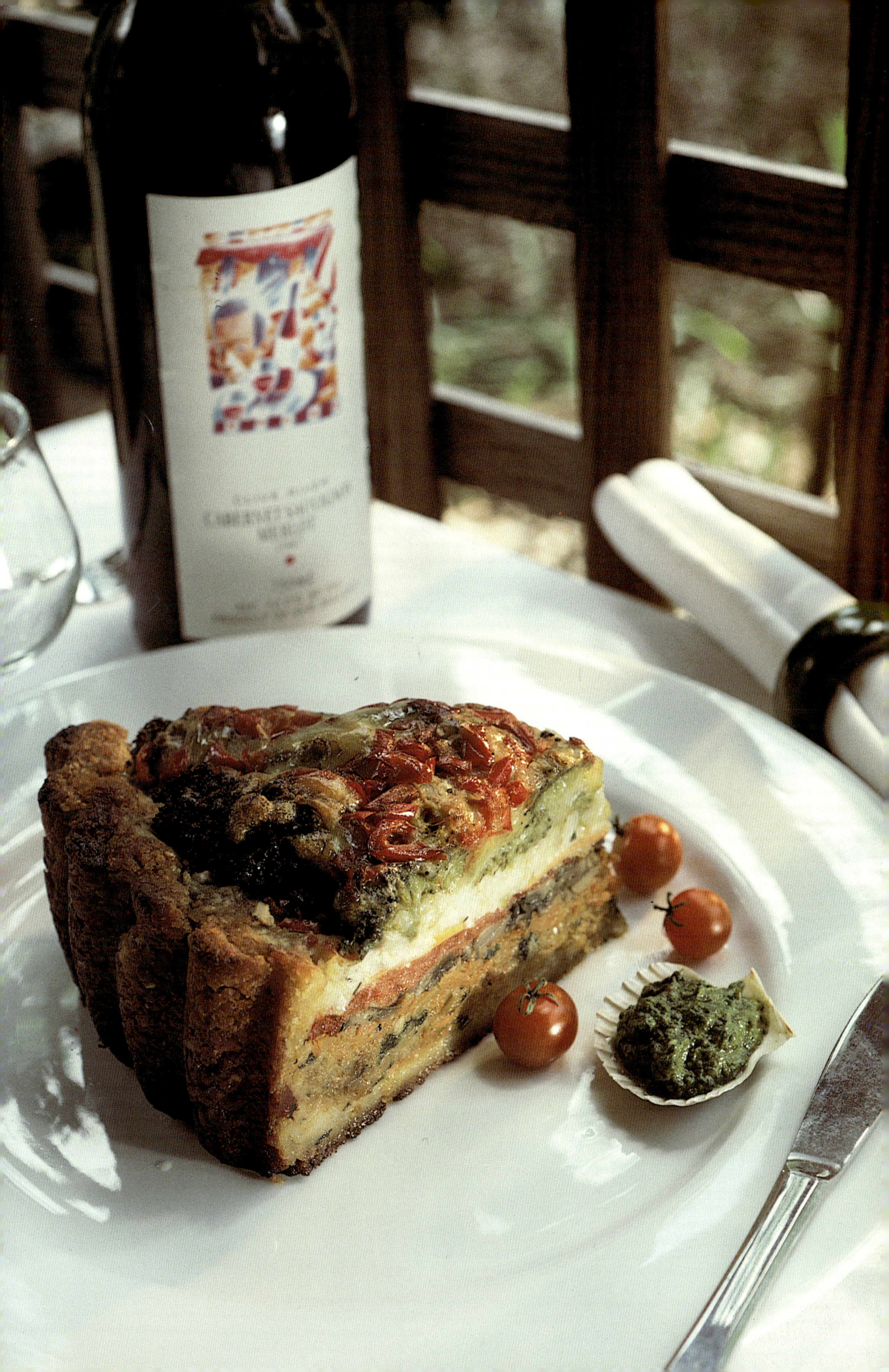

Uniquely Australian

Vegetarian lasagna

To serve 1

2 slices young eggplant
2 slices medium ripe tomato
4 slices mushroom
12 slices medium zucchini
¼ cup grated mozzarella
ground bush tomatoes
butter for frying
bush tomato sauce

Prepare the sauce as described below but well in advance as the flavour strengthens over time. Separately, pan fry the sliced eggplant, tomato, mushroom and zucchini in butter until just soft. Arrange in lasagne fashion using ground bush tomatoes for seasoning. Bake in a hot oven for 10 minutes. Cover with grated cheese and grill to brown the cheese. Heat the sauce and spoon onto the lasagna and then finish with a sprinkle of ground bush tomato.

Bush tomato sauce

¼ cup bush tomatoes
½ cup red wine
1 small onion
1 red capsicum
100ml cream

Marinate the bush tomatoes in red wine for 24 hours.
Roughly chop the onion and capsicum and combine them with the bush tomatoes and cream.
Reduce the sauce and then purée to smoothness.

Try this recipe with bush tomato lasagna pasta layered between the vegetable layers or with any of your favourite pastas. Add or replace any vegetables as desired.

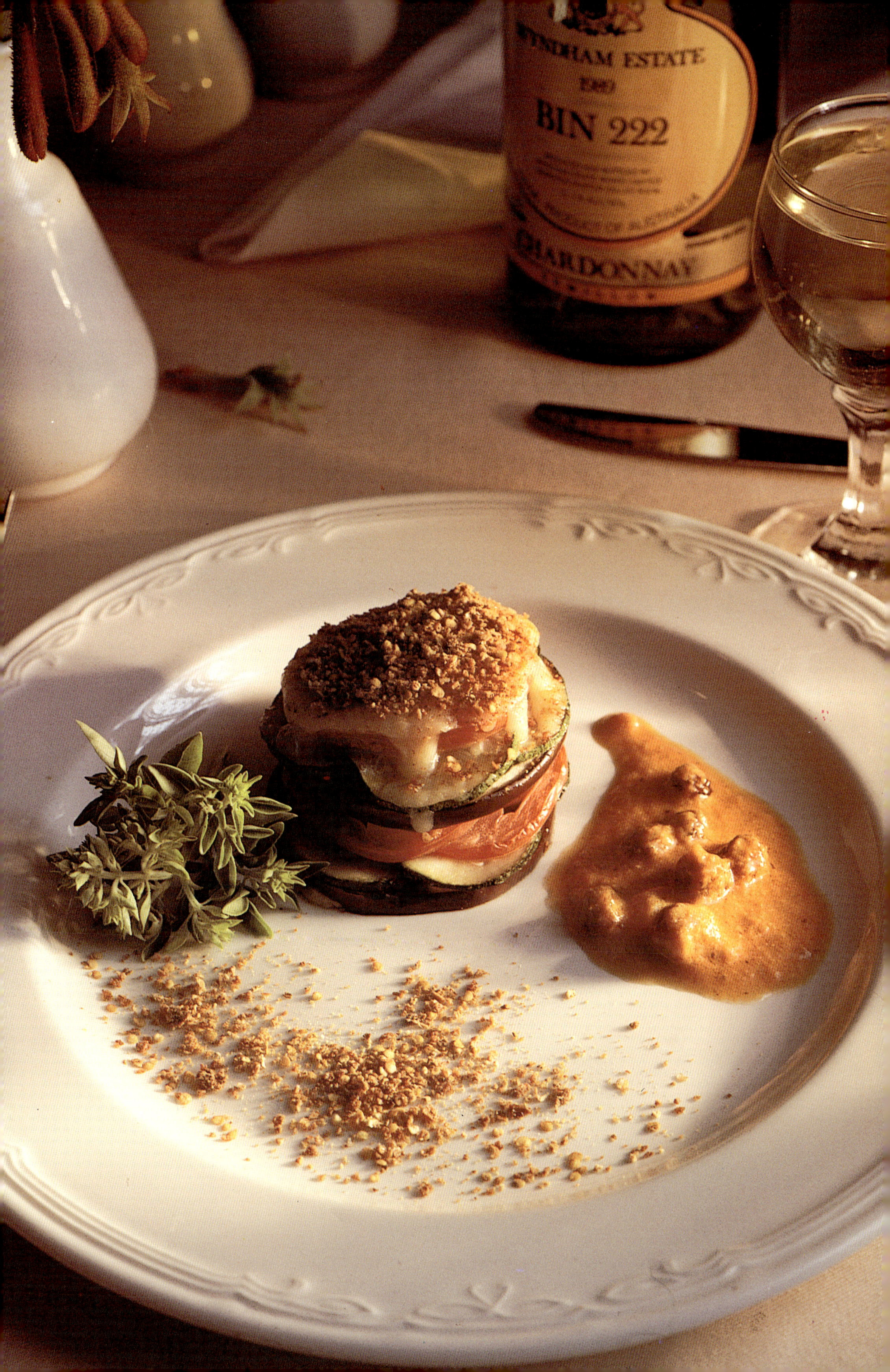
ESTATE
BIN 222

Uniquely Australian

Clay rack of lamb

To serve 1

**4 bone rack per person
1 drop food grade eucalyptus oil
½ cup macadamia oil
½ teaspoon rosemary
½ teaspoon thyme
seasonings**

Add the eucalyptus oil to the macadamia oil and rub them onto the lamb racks. Sprinkle on the herbs and seasonings and refrigerate overnight. In a hot oiled pan, sear the rack to seal the meat then place it into a hot oven for 5 minutes. Allow to cool. Using potter's clay, wrap the rack with the ribs protruding. Bake the rack for 30 minutes at 300°C.

If the earthy flavour of the clay is not to your taste, wrap the rack in paperbark or a good quality greaseproof or silicone paper before encasing it in the clay.

Uniquely Australian

Uniquely Australian

Riberry quail

To serve 4

8 quail
seasonings
1 tablespoon macadamia oil
2 cups riberries
2 cups chicken stock
1 small onion, finely diced

Season the inside of each quail and then rub the outside with oil. Brown gently in a lightly oiled fry pan for about 5 minutes then roast in a moderate oven for 15 minutes. Set the quail aside.
To the pan juices add the onion and fry until tender. Add the stock and reduce the volume by half. Crush most of the riberries leaving a handful whole. Add the crushed fruits to the stock, cover the pan and continue to reduce until it almost forms a glaze. Remove the pan from the heat and strain. Add the whole riberries and serve over the quail.

Riberries or clove lillipillies are best if seedless. A naturally occurring variety produces strongly flavoured fruits with seeds in only about 5% of fruits. It is this variety which is being propagated in preference to the more common seeded form.

Uniquely Australian

Uniquely Australian

Kangaroo fillet with quandong chilli sauce

To serve 1

200g trimmed kangaroo fillet
macadamia nut oil
seasoning

Brush the kangaroo meat with oil, season and char-grill or pan fry to rare or medium rare. Rest the meat in a warm place for 10 to 15 minutes before carving.

Quandong chilli sauce

10 to 15g dried quandongs
½ cup port
¼ cup red wine vinegar
2 cups rich meat stock
chopped fresh chilli to taste

Soak the quandongs in the port for 15 minutes. Pour off the port into a frying pan. Reduce the port and vinegar together until syrupy. Add the stock and reduce by half, skimming frequently. Add the quandongs (allowing 6 to 8 pieces of fruit per person). Add the chilli and simmer for 5 minutes before serving.

Uniquely Australian

To stew dried quandongs, simply soak them for 15 minutes in apple or pear juice or for a sweeter finish, in juice concentrate. A dash of orange liqueur can also be added to good effect. Bring the softened quandongs to the boil and gently poach for no longer than 5 minutes. Refrigerate overnight before use to enhance the flavour.

Lamb loin with bunya nuts and warrigal greens

To serve 4

1 boned loin of lamb with flap
200g bunya nuts, boiled and shelled
150g warrigal greens, blanched and drained
2 eggs
½ teaspoon Dijon mustard
1 cup white breadcrumbs
garlic and seasonings

Squeeze the warrigal greens of excess moisture and blend them with the eggs, mustard, breadcrumbs and garlic. Season to taste. Roughly chop the bunya nuts and add them to the mix. Roll the mixture into a sausage shape as long as the lamb loin using paperbark or baking paper and aluminium foil. Add extra breadcrumbs if the mixture is too loose to roll. Poach the roll in a water bath in a moderate oven for 15 minutes. Refresh the roll in iced water and unwrap it. Set aside.
Trim the loin of excess fat and sinew, lay it out and roll up around the warrigal and bunya nut filling. Tie up the roll with string and roast it to medium rare in a hot oven.

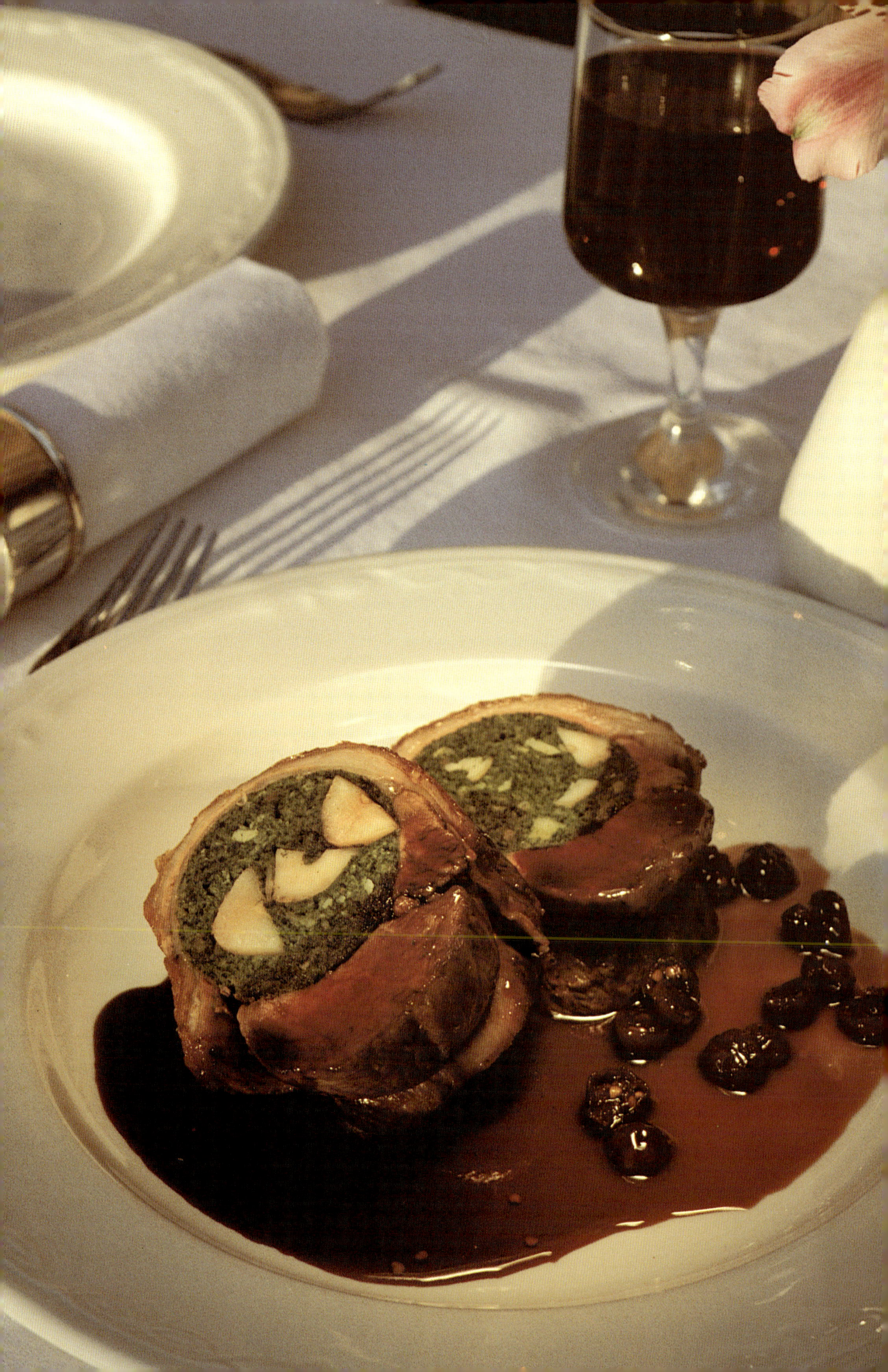

Seared emu medallions

To serve 2

**300g emu saddle, cut into medallions
clarified butter for frying
⅓ cup (50g) dried quandongs
½ cup apple juice
1 teaspoon lemon juice
4 teaspoons boysenberry purée
6 native pepper leaves
½ cup thickened cream
seasonings**

Soak the quandong in the apple juice to soften (about 15 minutes). Melt the clarified butter in a very hot pan and sear the emu medallions. Remove the emu from the pan to a hot plate. Rest the meat for 15 minutes. Reduce the heat, add the quandong and juice and the remaining ingredients. Reduce the mixture to thicken and serve over the emu medallions.

Marinated kangaroo kurrajong

To serve 2

**200g kangaroo fillet, cut into medallions
500ml macadamia oil
1 clove garlic
½ cup kurrajong flour
100g Kakadu plums
½ cup munthari berries
6 lemon myrtle leaves
1 tablespoon lemon juice
¼ cup meat stock
½ cup thickened cream
seasonings**

Combine the oil, garlic and munthari and cover the meat in this marinade overnight. Remove the fillets and allow to drain. Dust both sides of the fillets with kurrajong flour and fry in a very hot oiled pan until sealed on both sides. Set the meat aside to rest. Add the remaining ingredients to the pan juices and reduce to thicken. Season and serve over the meat.

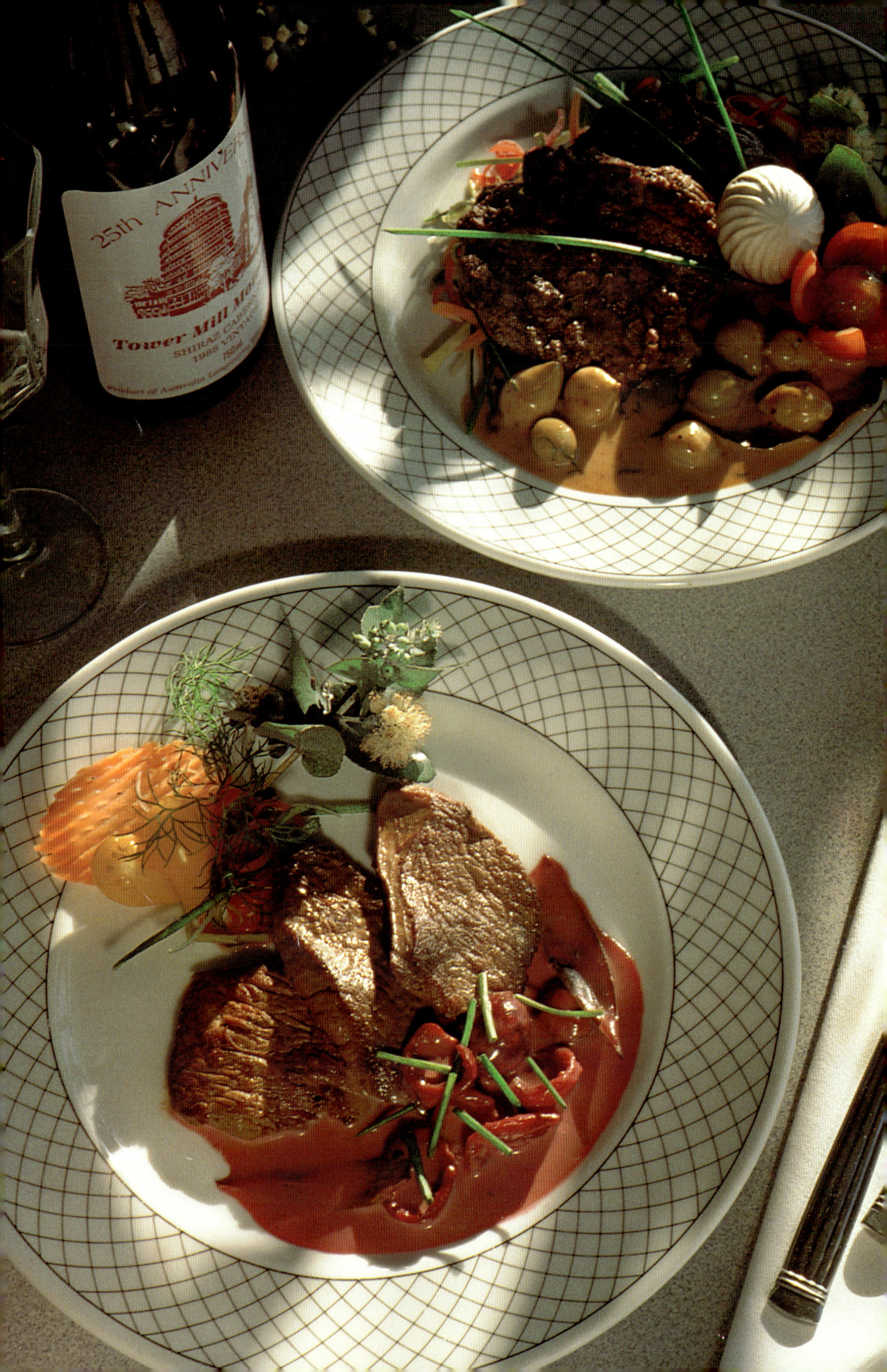
25th
Tower Mill
SHIRAZ

Uniquely Australian

Capretto goat with native pepperleaf sauce

To serve 2

360g Capretto goat (boneless saddle)
60g yams or white sweet potato
seasoning
macadamia oil for frying

Native pepperleaf sauce

½ cup brown stock
1½ tablespoons butter
6 native pepper leaves

Heat macadamia oil to smoking and sear both sides of the goat saddle.
Set the meat aside in a warm place to rest and finish cooking.
Reduce the stock by half and gently fold in butter.
Grind the pepperleaves to a fine powder in an electric coffee grinder.
Remove the sauce from the heat and add the pepper.

To serve, slice the goat saddle into 8 pieces and arrange 4 pieces per plate with the sauce mirrored underneath. Garnish with steamed yam batons and vegetables of the season.

The three species of native pepper available commercially are distinctly different in flavour. Snow pepper has a banana character, mountain pepper has overtones of bayleaf and Dorrigo pepper is the hottest of the three. Each pepper tends to lose its zing after being ground (they will last about 3 weeks in an airtight jar) or if overcooked. Used like a bayleaf and stewed the flavours are retained even if the zing disappears. To keep the peppery zing add the pepper to the dish after cooking. Try native pepper with conventional pepper steak.

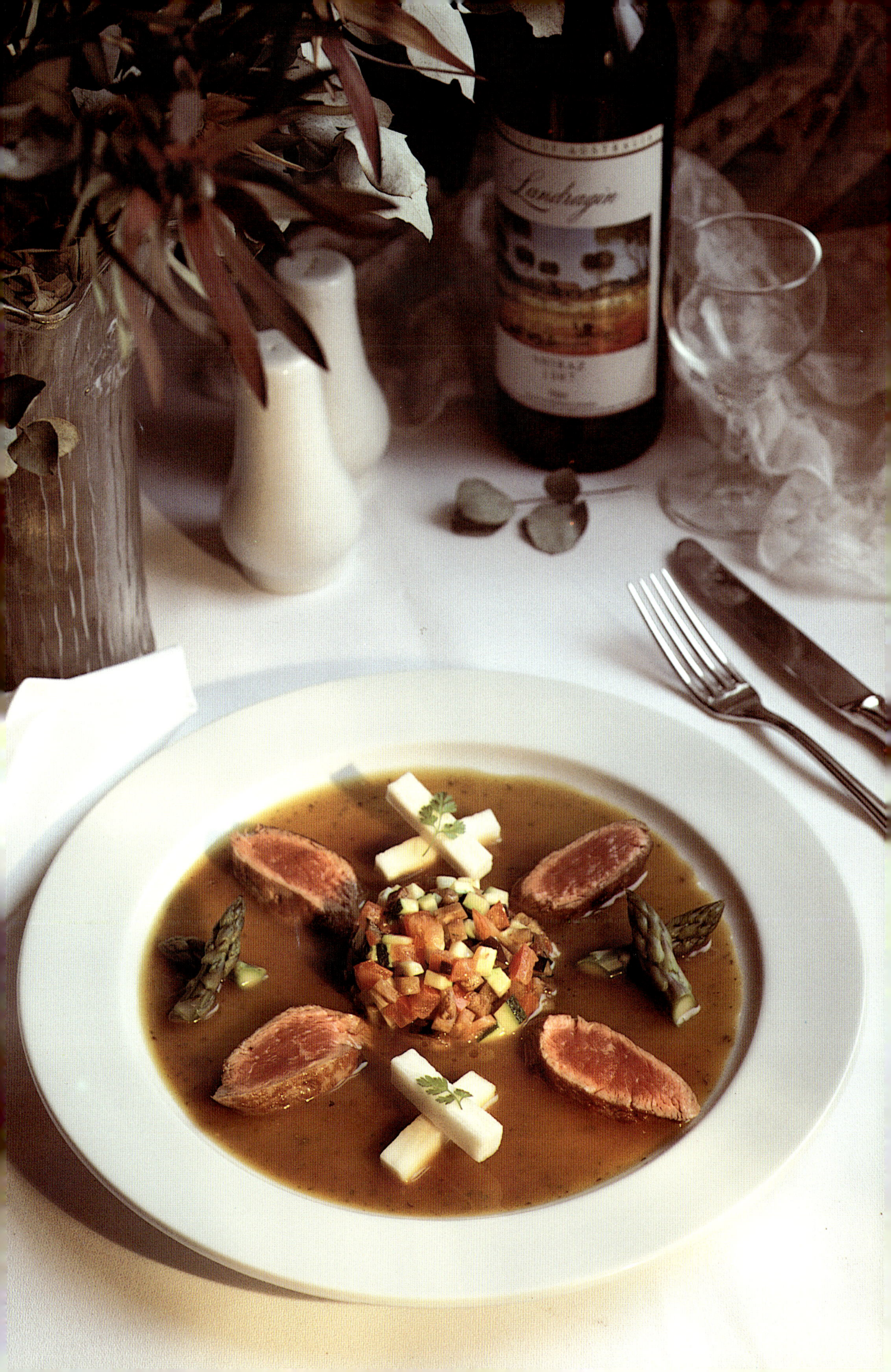
Landragin

Bush fired water buffalo tenderloin

Serves 4

4 x 180g water buffalo tenderloin
1½ tablespoons macadamia oil
seasoning

Lightly brush the buffalo steaks with macadamia oil and season the meat. Cook to just medium-rare over a very hot char-grill. Rest the meat in a warm place to finish cooking.

Ragout of warrigal greens

120g warrigal greens, blanched and coarsely chopped
¼ cup beef stock
¼ cup cream
seasoning

Reduce the stock by half in a small saucepan and then add the cream. Bring the stock back to the boil, season and stir in the chopped warrigal greens.

Confit

8 cloves of garlic
8 pieces eschallot onions
60g butter
⅔ cup sugar

Blanch garlic and onions in salted water. Place butter and sugar in a saucepan and caramelise. Add onions and garlic and leave for 2 hours.

Sauce

1 small onion, finely chopped
1¾ cups red wine
sprig of fresh thyme
¼ cup port
¼ cup red wine vinegar
1¼ cup chicken stock
½ cup beef stock
½ tablespoon cold butter
1½ tablespoons rosella jam

Marinate onions, red wine, thyme, port and vinegar for 12 hours. Bring to the boil and reduce by two thirds. Remove the thyme. Combine both stocks and reduce slowly by half. Blend in cold butter and rosella jam. Season the sauce to taste.

Garnish

12 rosella flowers
2 small mushrooms, diced

To serve, place the ragout in the centre of each plate. Cut each steak into 8 slices and fan the slices over the ragout. Scatter diced mushrooms around the outer edge of the plate and place 2 garlic pieces and 2 onion pieces in between. Spoon the sauce over and around the meat. Garnish with rosella flowers and fresh herbs.

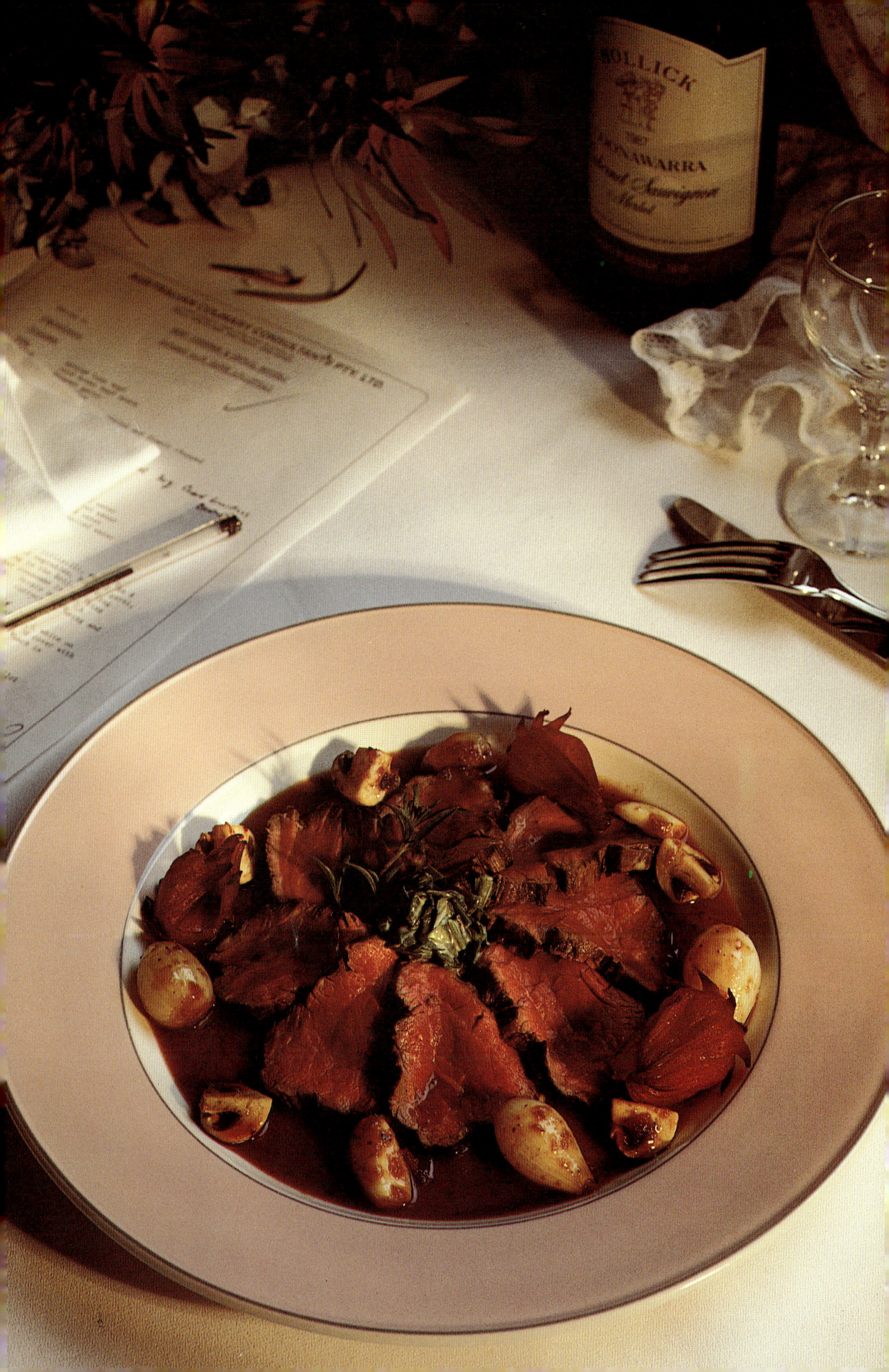

Uniquely Australian

Smoked emu

To serve 4

**100g sliced smoked emu saddle
½ cup macadamia nut oil
1 drop food grade eucalyptus oil
several wild limes, halved
1 tomato, sliced
1 onion, chopped
some vegetables cut into strips
some salad lettuce**

Arrange the slices of emu on each plate.
Add the eucalyptus oil to the macadamia nut oil.
Garnish each plate and drizzle the emu slices with the oil.

Emus are now farmed in Western Australia and Queensland. Feathers, leather, oil and several other products are marketed as well as the meat. Unfortunately, passive farming is not supported by wildlife authorities and the birds tend to be intensively raised rather than free ranged and humanely wild harvested.

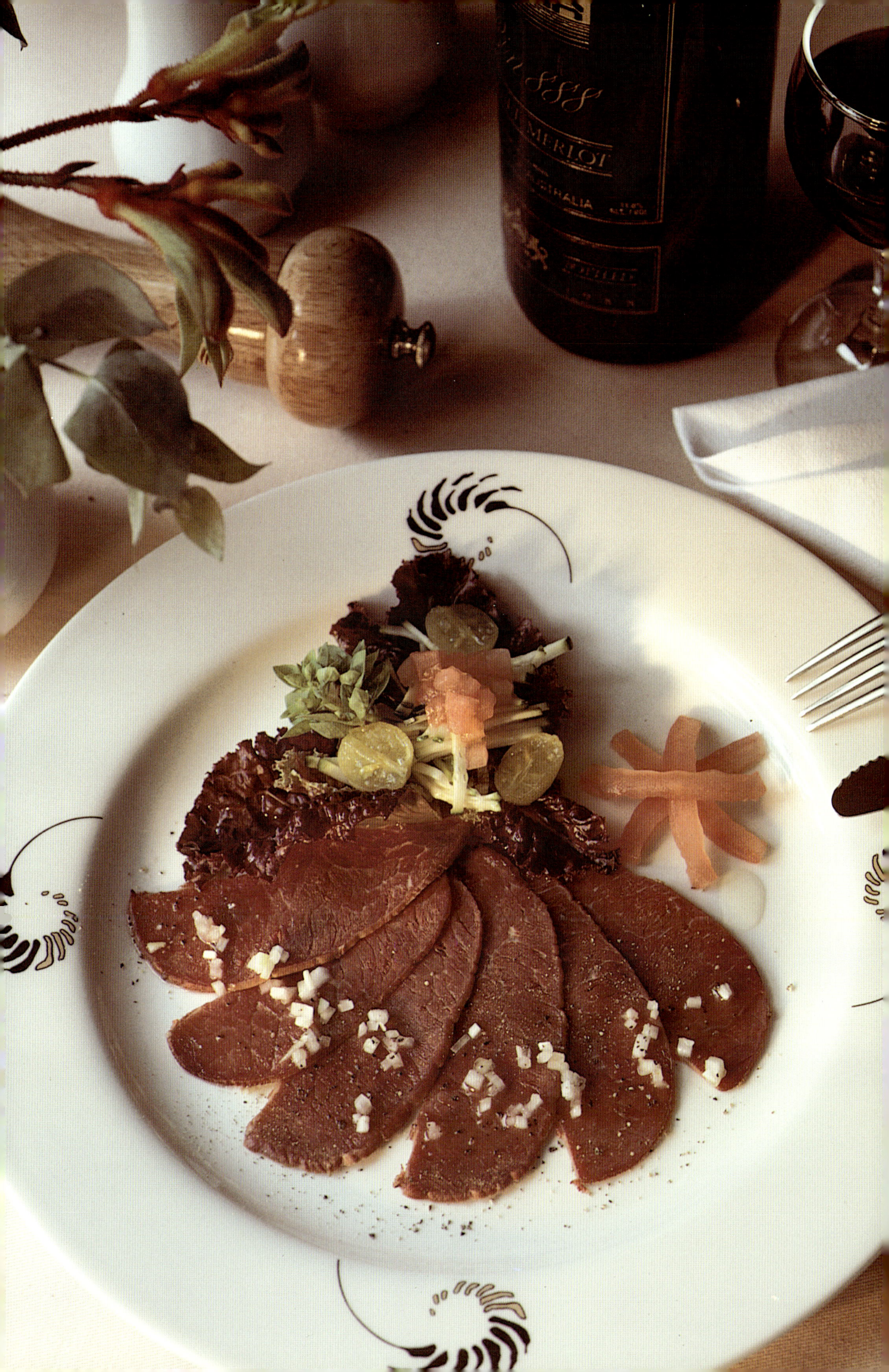
MERLOT

Uniquely Australian

Beef tenderloin with quandong

To serve 2

**200g beef tenderloin, centre cut
½ cup reduced beef stock
½ litre red wine
¼ cup quandong, pre-soaked in ½ cup of orange juice.
1 large savoury cabbage leaf, poached
2 native pepper leaves
¼ cup bush tomatoes
parsley
carrot trims**

Simmer the tenderloin for 15 minutes in the stock and wine. Cook to medium rare. Remove the meat from the liquor and wrap it in the blanched cabbage leaf. Set it aside in a warm place to finish cooking. Add the orange juice from the softened quandongs to the pan (reserving the fruit) and add the pepperleaf. Cover the pan and heat to reduce the volume by two thirds. Pass through a sieve. Put back onto the heat and add the reserved pieces of softened quandong. Simmer for 5 minutes.

To serve, spoon on the sauce and quandong fruits onto two plates. Slice the beef into four pieces and arrange two pieces on each plate. Finish by garnishing with the bush tomatoes, parsley and carrot trims.

The quandong is well known throughout South Australia but quandongs are also found in New South Wales and Western Australia. Some quandongs are sweet while others are too bitter to eat without preparation, some trees produce edible seed kernels while other seeds have medicinal kernels. Aborigines also know never to shelter under a quandong tree in a thunderstorm since the trees tend to attract lightning.

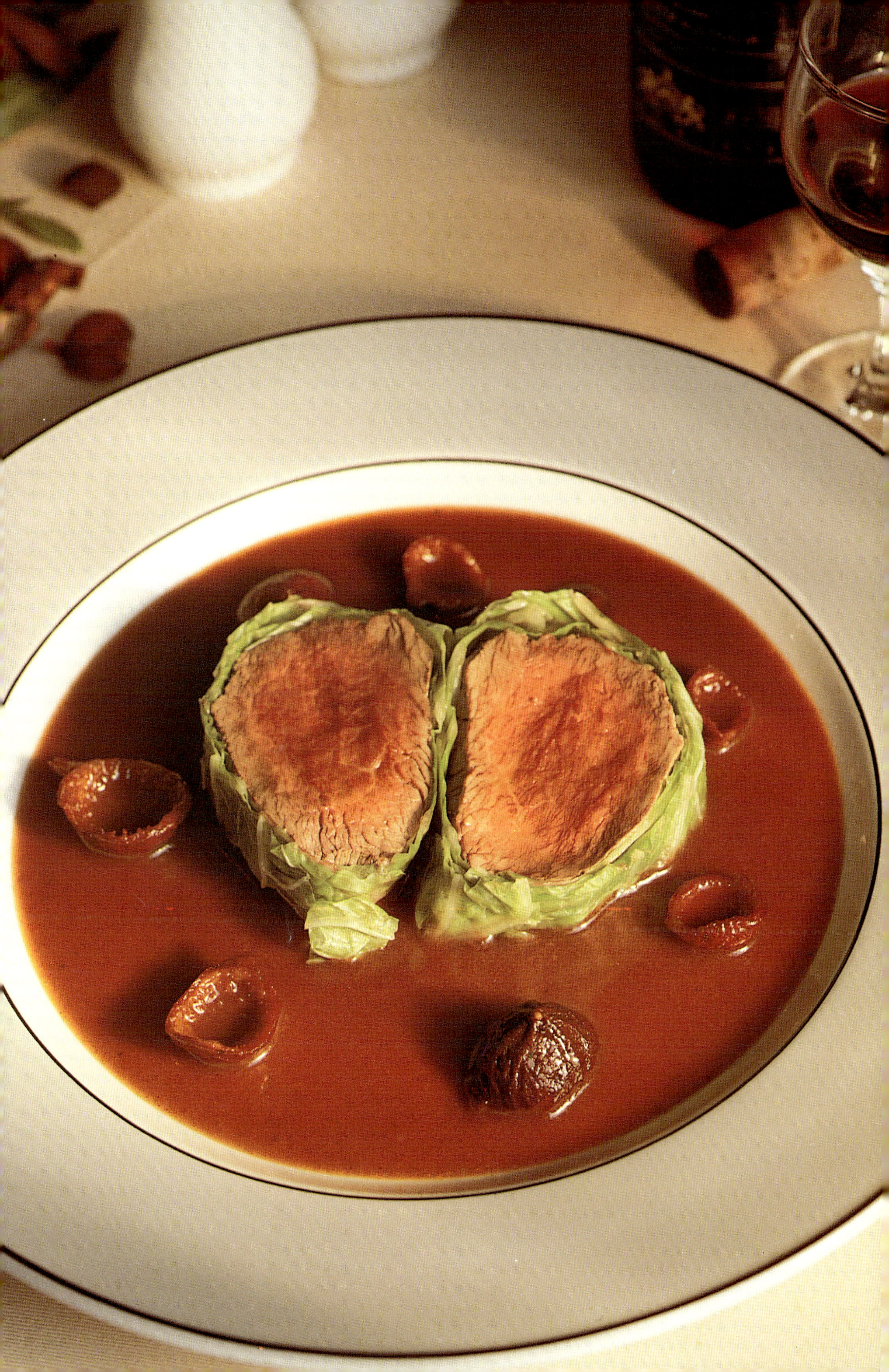

Uniquely Australian

Lamb cutlet duet

To serve 2

Cutlets

1 rack of lamb, cut into 4 cutlets
¼ cup kurrajong flour
1 egg, beaten
¼ cup macadamia nuts, finely chopped
1 tablespoon wattle
macadamia oil for frying
1 tablespoon unsalted butter

Hollandaise

3 egg yolks
2 teaspoons white wine
250g clarified butter
1 sprig of lemon tea tree, chopped

Dust cutlets in kurrajong flour, dip in egg and then coat two with either wattle or macadamia nuts. Panfry in hot oil and butter until the macadamia cutlets are golden brown. Both crumbed cutlets will then be done. Finish in a hot oven at 250°C for 5 minutes. Make the hollandaise by whipping egg yolks and wine in a double boiler. Continue whipping while adding clarified butter and the lemon tea tree.

Serve one of each cutlet and a little of the sauce with a variety of seasonal vegetables. The sauce can also be offered in a jug.

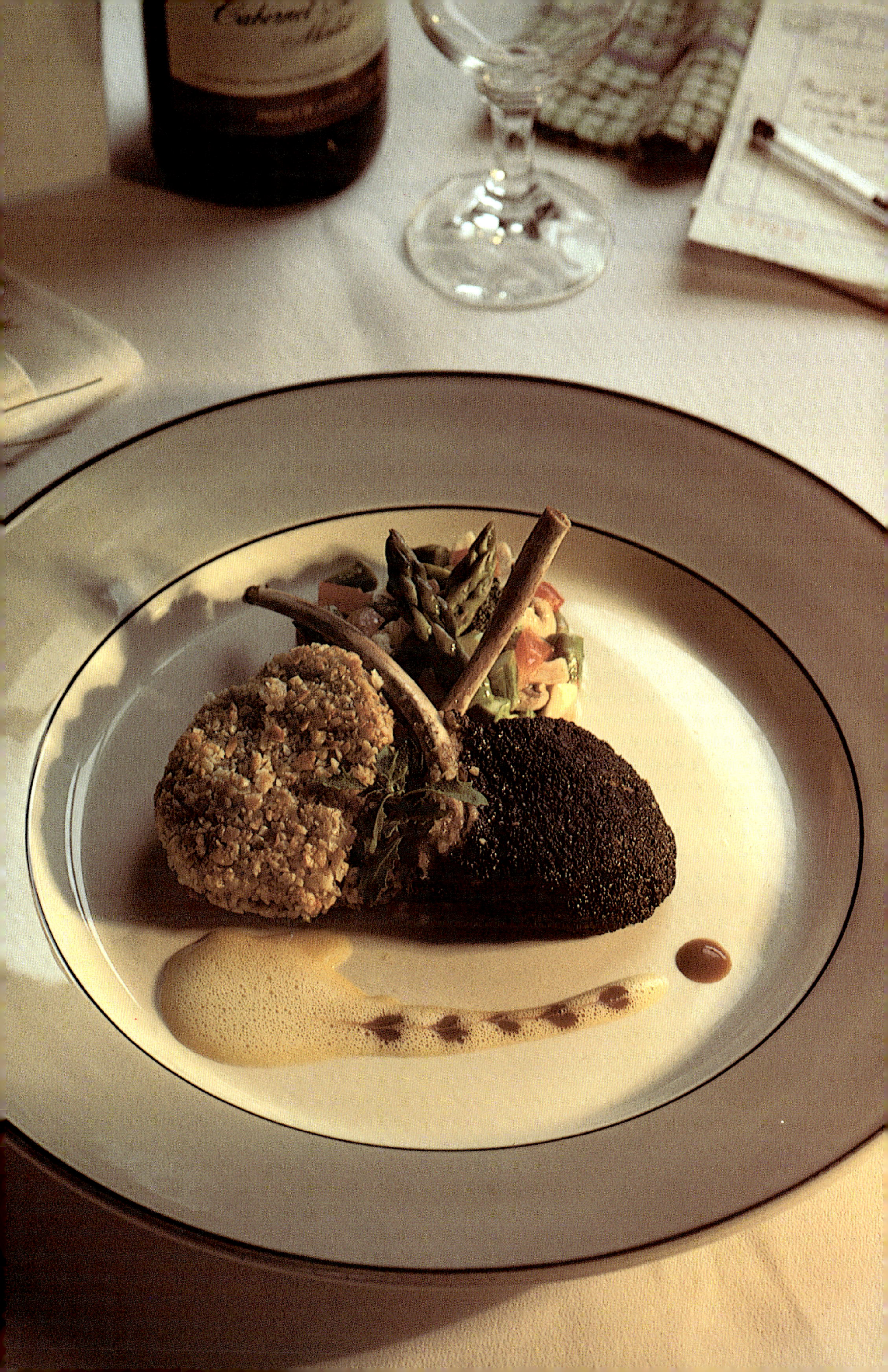

Bunya nut smoked mutton salad

To serve 4

1 x 240g mutton backstrap
120g mixed lettuce salad eg. cos, mignonette, oakleaf,
whitlof, mache, raddichio
8 orange segments
8 lemon aspen, halved and soaked in honey syrup
8 snow peas, thinly sliced
1 red capsicum thinly sliced
fresh chervil to garnish

Sear the mutton backstrap for 5 minutes each side on a char-grill over smoking bunya nut shells, wood and sawdust. (Soak the shells and wood in water overnight to provide the smoke). Transfer the meat to a warm oven tray and place some of the smoking bunya wood around the meat. Cover and leave aside to rest.

Eucalyptus and lemon aspen vinaigrette

500ml salad oil
¾ teaspoon food grade eucalyptus oil
2 teaspoons lemon aspen juice

Combine the ingredients and blend or whisk. Mix well again just before using. Store leftover vinaigrette in the refrigerator for up to six months.

Arrange the salad leaves in the centre of 4 round plates.
Place the citrus segments around the edge of each portion.
Cut the warm backstrap into thin slices and place evenly over the salads.
Drizzle on the vinaigrette and garnish with the chervil.

Uniquely Australian

There are many native woods which can be used to impart their characteristic flavours to meats and vegetables. Take some care with the cones of banksias. They tend to give a bitter taste once the food cools.

Paperbark baked lamb with bunya nut purée and wild fruit chutney

To serve 2

180g lamb loin
½ cup bunya nut purée
2 leaves of native mint
paperbark
vine for tying
macadamia oil for frying

Sear the seasoned lamb in hot macadamia oil. Allow to cool. Finely chop the mint and fork it through the bunya nut purée. Spread the purée over the seared loin. Wrap the meat in paperbark, tie it with a length of green vine and bake in a hot oven at 250°C for 10 minutes. Rest the meat briefly before serving. Unwrap the paperbark parcel at the table.

Wild fruit chutney

1 medium black apple
6 Illawarra plums, cores removed
20ml lemon aspen juice
10ml sugarbag

To prepare the chutney, coarsely chop the black apples and Illawarra plums. Removing the cores of the plums lessens the chance of the plums being astringent or bitter. Combine the chopped fruits with the remaining ingredients and serve.

Black apples are difficult fruits with which to cook. If the fruits are boiled they go very hard rather than cooking down to a pulp. One way around this problem is to freeze and then thaw the fruits to get a soft, 'cooked' purée.

Uniquely Australian

Paperbark is an ideal food wrap since it is not toxic to eat even though it is indigestible. This requirement is necessary for restaurant use when serving food still wrapped in paperbark. Australian health authorities demand that everything served on a plate must be able to be consumed.

Uniquely Australian

Kangaroo broth and kurrajong dumplings

To serve 4

Broth

200g minced kangaroo meat
¼ cup riberries
1 egg white
seasoning
1 1itre of kangaroo meat stock
1 cup mixed vegetables, peeled and finely chopped
6 native pepper leaves
4 lemon myrtle leaves
a sprig of lemon tea tree
4 peppercorns
½ cup riberries, blended

Dumplings

⅔ cups cooked kangaroo tail meat diced
2 egg whites
1 cup kurrajong flour

Garnish

½ cup cooked kangaroo tail meat diced
8 seedless riberry fruit
8 carrot pieces turned
8 zucchini pieces turned
4 small shallots or native leak leaves

Uniquely Australian

Broth

Thoroughly mix the kangaroo meat, whole riberries, egg white, seasoning and a quarter of the cold stock in a thick bottomed saucepan. Add the vegetables, native herbs, peppercorns, blended riberries and remainder of the stock. With the saucepan covered, slowly bring the soup to the boil, stirring occasionally. Once boiling, move the saucepan to the side of the heat source and reduce the heat so that only half the pan is heated. Simmer for 1½ hours without stirring. Strain the soup through a doubled muslin cloth. Remove any fat with a ladle and correct the seasoning and colour. Set aside.

Dumplings

Beat the egg whites in a small bowl and thicken with kurrajong flour. Fold in the tail meat and add to boiling salted water by the spoonful to form dumplings. Simmer until the dumplings float.

Garnish

Cook the turned vegetables in salted water. Refresh them in cold water.

To serve, bring the clarified broth to the boil and evenly distribute the soup into bowls. Place the garnishes and 3 dumplings into each bowl. Serve immediately.

Uniquely Australian

Five star restaurant presentation of desserts can turn food into art.

Sweet things

Restaurant menus end with the desserts and yet many people often scan the sweet offerings first. Even reading a list of desserts stimulates appetite and urges further foraging through the starter and main course descriptions. It is a response to the instinctive taste drives for fat and sweetness. However, for good nutrition, the urge to satisfy this drive must be moderated and the intake of fats and refined sugar reduced.

Almost the entire range of bushfoods commercially available is particularly well suited to desserts. The citrus characteristics or the subtle stone fruit flavours of bush fruits, that elusive taste often described simply as nuttiness in many of the seeds and nuts, the many spice-like qualities similar to cinnamon, cloves and aniseed in bush fruits and herbs and the uniquely Australian flavour of resinous pine and eucalyptus are all enhanced in sweet dishes. It is interesting to note that cane sugar is often overly strong in its own flavour to bring out the best in many bushfoods. Honey and fruit concentrates merge better with subtle characteristics and can provide additional nutrients, mainly minerals and fibre. Refined fructose can be used as another alternative and since it is sweeter than the equivalent amount of cane sugar, total food energy can be beneficially reduced.

The following recipes range from high sugar to only unrefined sweetener desserts. Remember that all food is nutritious but all nutrients can be toxic if their concentration is too high. The secret is moderation and variety. If cane sugar and fats are essential for the recipe as in pavlovas and ice creams then eat less and less often. With fruit concentrates just as with cane sugar, sucrose is still the dominant sweetener and this should be considered in a balanced diet.

Use the recipes as presented or as a guide in modifying sugared dishes into naturally sweetened ones. Compare the flavours of the same dish made with different sweeteners and make your own choice. All food but particularly dessert, is meant to be enjoyed, so enjoy it!

Chocolate and wattle mousse

⅓ cup (50g) wattle
100ml water
375g good quality dark (couverture) chocolate
3 egg yolks
125ml milk
375ml cream
3 egg whites
2 tablespoons castor sugar

Make a wattle essence by boiling the wattle in water. Strain the essence. The grounds are no longer needed for this recipe but store them frozen for later use in other recipes. Whisk the yolks, milk and the prepared wattle essence over a water bath until the mixture thickens. Melt the chocolate over a water bath and fold into the wattle mixture. Use couverture chocolate to ensure a well set mousse. Allow to cool to room temperature. Whip cream to the soft to medium peak stage. Whip the egg whites and sugar also to the same stage. If the whites and cream are over-whipped they are more difficult to fold into the chocolate mix and the mousse tends to be lumpy. Fold in one third of the cream and whites, then when almost incorporated, fold in the remaining two thirds of each. Chill. Serve with brandy snaps or a tuile over a native fruit purée or alternatively, over the commercially produced Kakadu plum jelly, diluted to a thick sauce with water.

Native fruit purée

3 apples, stewed
juice of any native fruit eg. lemon aspen, native limes

The apples can be cooked whole since they will be strained later. Blend the cooked apples to a purée. Add sufficient of the wild fruit juice to flavour the apple and then push the mix through a sieve or wring it through muslin to yield a smooth sauce.

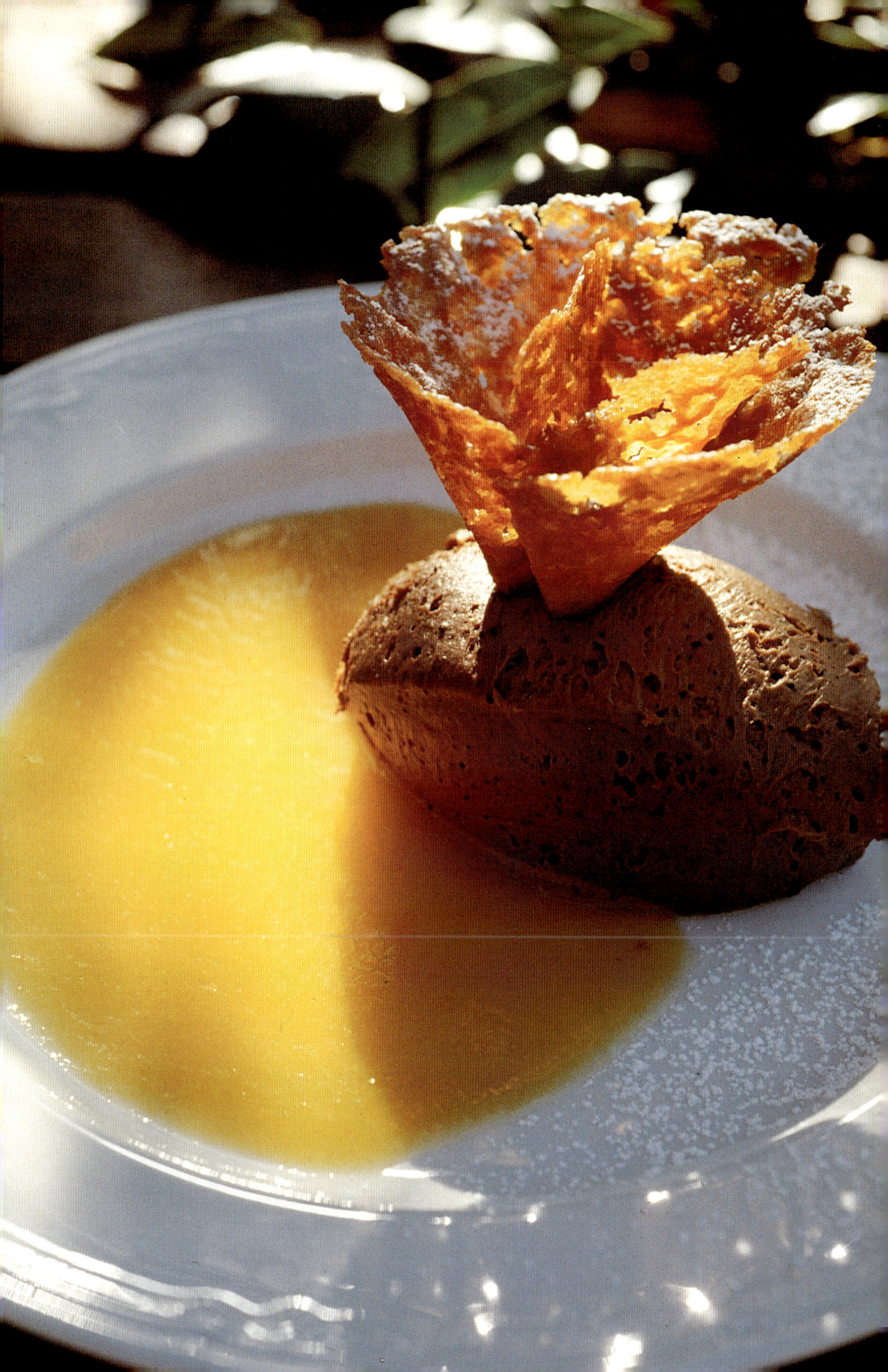

Riberry bread and butter pudding

150g butter
¼ cup sugar
250ml milk
100ml cream
2 drops pure vanilla essence
¼ cup riberries
¼ cup macadamia nuts, roasted and chopped
15 slices of bread without the crusts

Cream the butter and sugar until smooth. Add the milk, cream and vanilla. Into buttered molds or a muffin tray, place layers of bread triangles, riberries and chopped macadamia nuts finishing with bread and a few extra riberries. Pour the custard mix to the top of each mold. Add a dob of butter and a sprinkle of cinnamon onto each pudding. Put the molds into a large baking tray containing boiling water and cover over with an inverted baking tray. If using aluminium foil rather than an inverted tray, make sure it does not come in contact with the puddings (see below). Bake at 190°C for about 20 minutes over boiling water. Remove the covering tray or foil 5 minutes before removing the puddings from the oven. Allow to cool before removing puddings from molds.

Cooking with aluminium foil can often result in plastic meals. Aluminium foil is metal in a plastic sandwich. The plastic coating readily dissolves in the fats in foods leaving the foil dull as the aluminium is oxidised from exposure to air. Aluminium has also been shown to be in high concentrations in the brain tissues of sufferers of Alzheimer's disease.

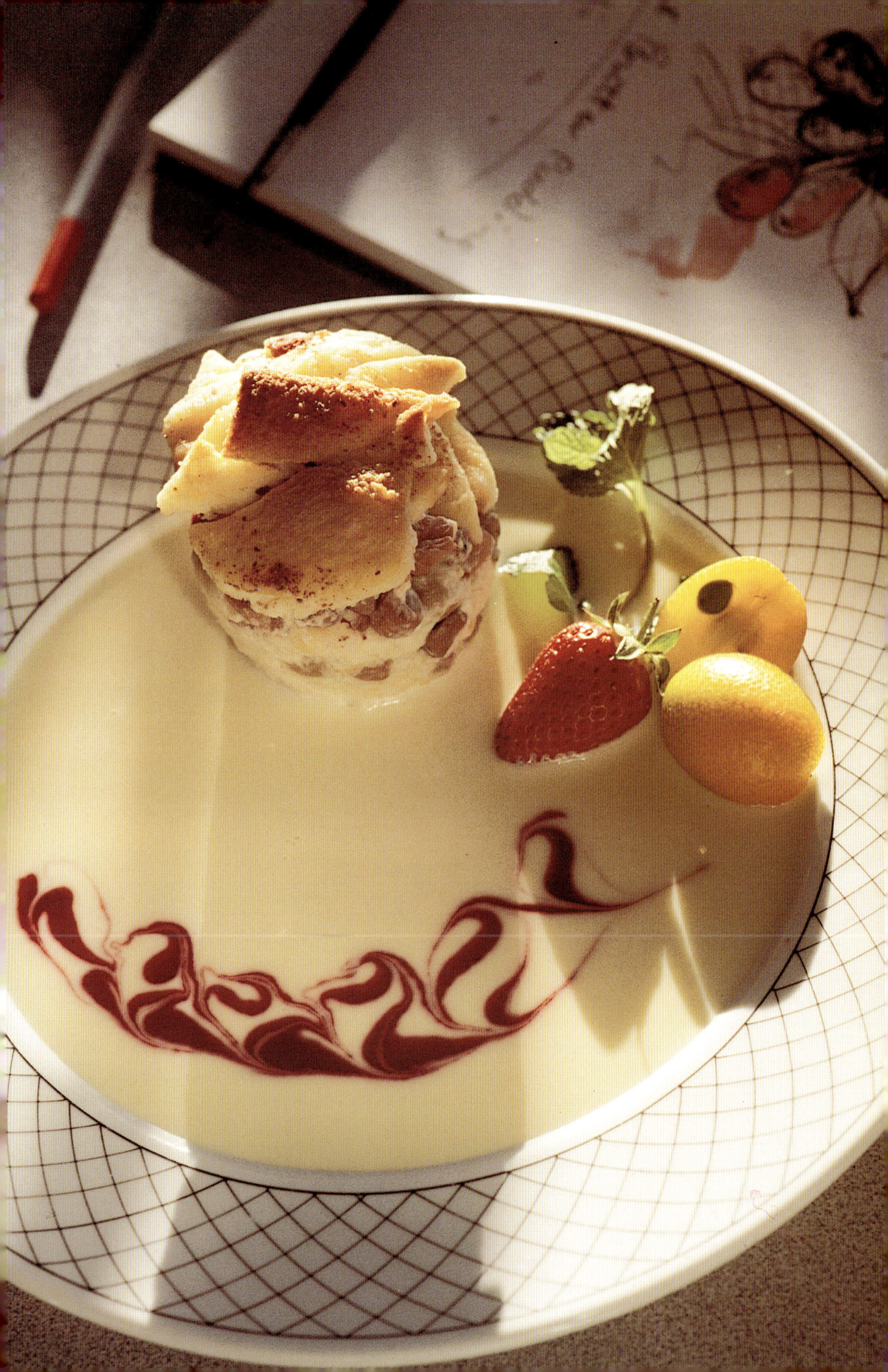

Uniquely Australian

Aussie Bush bomb

Flavourings

Wattle

**100ml water
1 tablespoon sugar
1 tablespoon wattle**

Combine all the ingredients and bring to the boil.

Eucalyptus

**1 teaspoon food grade eucalyptus oil
2 tablespoons pure bush honey
100ml water**

Combine and stir to dissolve the honey.

Ice cream

**1 cup milk
2 cups cream
3 egg yolks
¾ cup sugar
1 tablespoon glucose syrup
flavouring**

To make the ice creams, the above quantity of ice cream mix is needed for each flavour. Combine the base mix and flavouring. Heat to 81°C then chill and churn in an ice cream machine. Repeat for the second flavouring.

To assemble the bomb:

**wattle ice cream
eucalyptus and honey ice cream
Vienna chocolate cake, sliced
garnishing**

Use 9cm stainless steel dariole molds which have been chilled in the freezer. Spoon in the wattle ice cream and shape to form a 2cm thick shell of ice-cream formed up to the rim. Fill with eucalyptus ice cream and top the mold with a 10mm layer of cake. Set the bomb in the freezer. Garnish a serving plate with a marzipan gum leaf coloured with green food colouring and flavoured with a hint of eucalyptus oil. Make the chocolate log garnish by melting 300g good quality cooking chocolate in a double boiler. Add 30ml rum and 30ml glucose syrup. Pipe into log shapes before the chocolate sets.

If an ice cream churn is unavailable, put the prepared mixes into the freezer, whipping them with an electric mixer at intervals during freezing.

This will produce a more coarse (less creamy) ice cream. Another alternative is to use a ready made vanilla ice cream. For 1 litre of vanilla ice cream, make a wattle concentrate without the sugar and using 1 tablespoon of wattle in 50ml water, bring to the boil and cool. Mix into the softened ice cream. For the eucalyptus flavouring simply use the straight eucalyptus oil into another litre of softened vanilla ice cream. Adjust the flavours to taste. The ice creams can be re-aerated by beating with an electric beater to put back some of the air lost on thawing. Refreeze both flavoured ice creams and once frozen, assemble the bush bomb as opposite.

Eucalyptus oil must always be used very sparingly to make the flavour an after-taste rather than an overwhelming medicinal one.

Uniquely Australian

Billy tea sorbet

1100ml water
½ cup tea
30g (a generous handful) lemon myrtle leaves
2½ cups (600g) sugar
¼ cup (75g) glucose syrup
1 lemon, juiced

Bring 600ml water to the boil. In half of this, steep the tea until the tea leaves begin to sink. Strain and leave the tea to cool. In the other 300ml of boiling water, steep the lemon myrtle leaving the leaves in the water until cold. In the remaining 500ml of cold water bring the sugar, glucose and lemon juice to the boil. Refrigerate. Combine the mixtures and churn in an ice cream and sorbet machine.

The lemon myrtle flavour of this dessert comes through
after the second or third mouthful of sorbet and well
after the first taste of the sweetened tea.

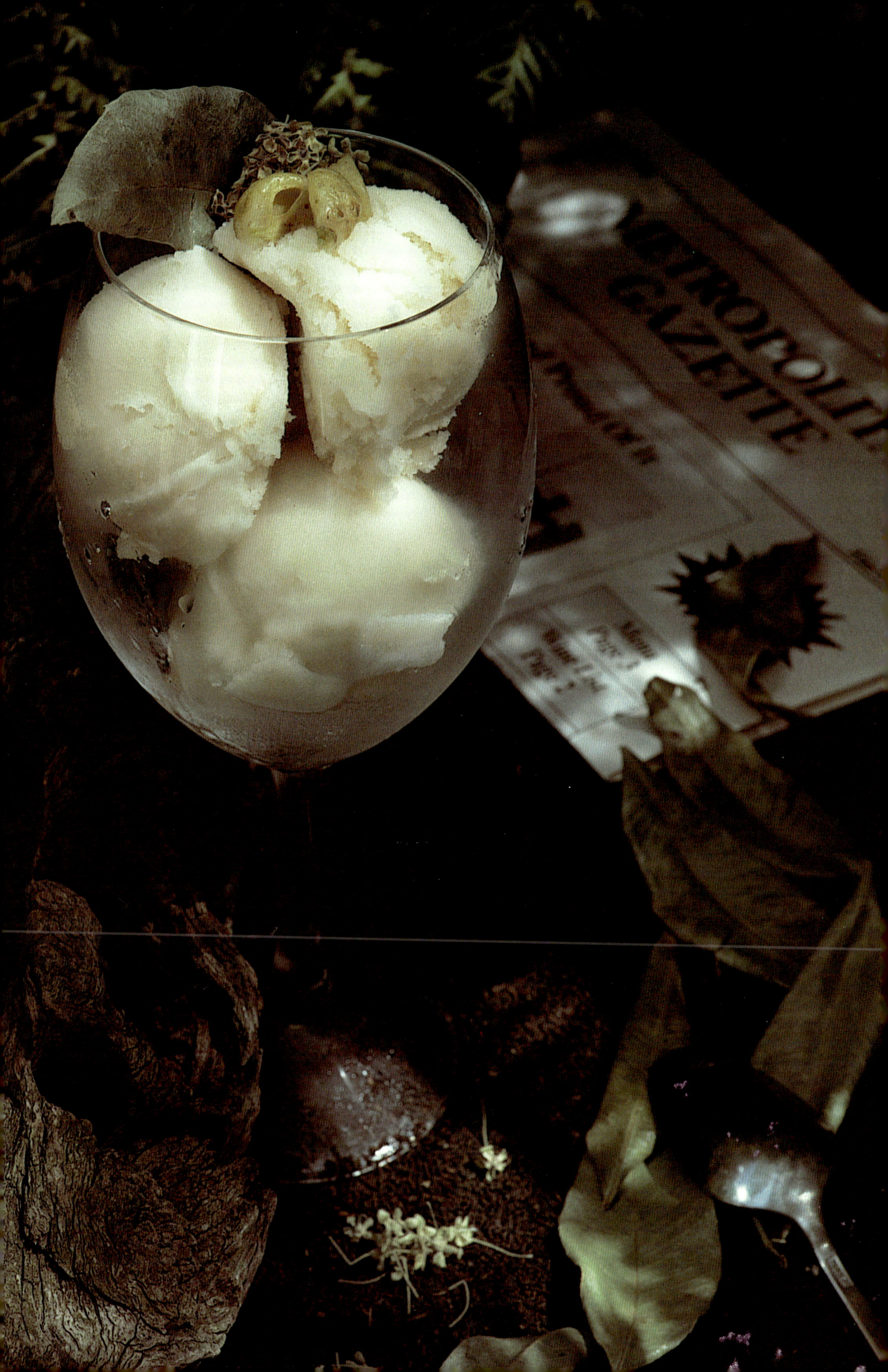
GAZETTE

Uniquely Australian

Bunya nut pudding

200g butter
1 cup sugar
6 eggs
1½ cups self raising flour
1¼ cups white bread crumbs
30ml golden syrup
125g bunya nuts, boiled, shelled and finely chopped
150ml milk
1½ cups apple, peeled and cooked,

Cream the butter and sugar. Mix in the eggs. Sift the flour and mix with the breadcrumbs then add this to the mixture. Fold in the remaining ingredients. Pour the mixture into buttered dariole molds and poach in a water bath for 40 minutes.
Serve with iced sugarbag and wattle sauce.

Wattle sauce

1 teaspoon wattle
2 tablespoons water
½ cup hulled tahini
2 tablespoons rice or barley malt

Bring all the ingredients to the boil and strain while boiling hot. The consistency can easily be changed by varying the amount of water. If necessary, re-warm to pour onto the bunya nut pudding.

This sauce can be used as a spread on toast and the grounds left in or used as a cake topping. Try using unhulled tahini for a slight bitterness or add a dash of flamed rum with or without cream as other options.

Bunya bunya nuts were once an important ceremonial food for Aboriginal groups living in north-east NSW and south-east Queensland. Bunya pines are large resinous trees and each third year produce a bumper crop of very large nut-bearing cones. Aborigines knew it was dangerous to camp under the trees since the falling cones left a lasting impression on human targets and during storms, the trees often attract lightning.

Uniquely Australian

Iced sugarbag

**3 egg yolks
2 cups of cream
1½ cups milk
½ cup sugar
vanilla bean, finely chopped
¾ cup sugarbag
1 tablespoon glucose syrup**

Warm all the ingredients except the sugarbag to 81°C. Chill, add the sugarbag and churn in an ice cream machine.

Sugarbag is an Aboriginal English word for the strong, bitter sweet honey from several species of Australian native bees. When cooking with sugarbag, remember that heat diminishes the unique flavour so reserve sugarbag for chilled desserts or serve it straight as a natural sauce.

Miner's fruit bag

filo pastry
butter
50g mixed dried fruits
50g mix of quandongs, Illawarra plums, munthari and riberries
30ml brandy (more or less to taste)
2 teaspoons honey or maple syrup

Melt the butter and brush onto a sheet of filo pastry. Repeat with another four sheets of pastry. Mix the fruits with a slug of brandy and the honey. Coarsely chop the fruits. Spoon out onto the pastry and wrap up the pastry to form the miner's bag. Bake at 160°C or until golden brown. Serve on top of a vanilla custard with wild rosella and native tamarind sauce. Garnish with riberries which have been soaked in maple syrup or glacéed in a sugar syrup.

Wild rosella and native tamarind sauce

25g wild rosellas
25g native tamarinds
50g pears, skinned and chopped
¼ cup port
maple syrup (optional)

Combine all the ingredients and lightly stew until the pears and wild fruits are cooked. Blend the mixture and strain through a muslin cloth. Sweeten to taste with maple syrup if desired. The sauce need not be strained but then core the pears ot remove the seeds.

Uniquely Australian

This miner's dessert is pure gold.

Rolled wattle and bunya nut pavlova

½ cup pavlova ready mix
250ml warm water
200g castor sugar
1 tablespoon drinking chocolate
½ cup mixed almonds and macadamia nuts, chopped (optional)

Meringue

Thoroughly mix the pavlova mix into the water and then beat for at least 6 to 8 minutes or until the mix forms very small bubbles and is a stiff whip. Add half the sugar and continue beating for 30 seconds. Spread the mix onto a sheet of silicone baking paper on a baking tray or a suitable piece of cardboard. Bake at 160°C for about 30 minutes or until only just sticky to touch but not browned. Cool. Mix the remaining castor sugar and drinking chocolate and the chopped nuts if desired, and sprinkle the mix over the pavlova. Flip the sugared pavlova onto a tea towel and spray the baking paper with water. Peel off the paper. Spread the filling over the pavlova to a ½cm thickness and roll it up using the tea towel as a guide. Refrigerate before serving.

Filling

Bunya nut and wattle cream

125g bunya nuts, boiled and shelled
2 tablespoons wattle
2 tablespoons maple syrup
500ml soy milk

Blend the bunya nuts in a food processor adding the soy milk slowly to assist the blending. Add the wattle and maple syrup and transfer the mixture to a saucepan. Heat to a simmer while stirring constantly until the mixture thickens to a whipped cream texture. Allow to cool and adjust the consistency with additional soy milk, if necessary. Stiffly whipped cream may be folded in at this stage if a lighter filling is desired.

This recipe is a dairy-free, low sugar modification to the emu egg pavlova presented in the Bush Food Handbook. The meringue mixes from either recipe can be interchanged, however, the wattle flavour is heightened if the sugar content is not too high.

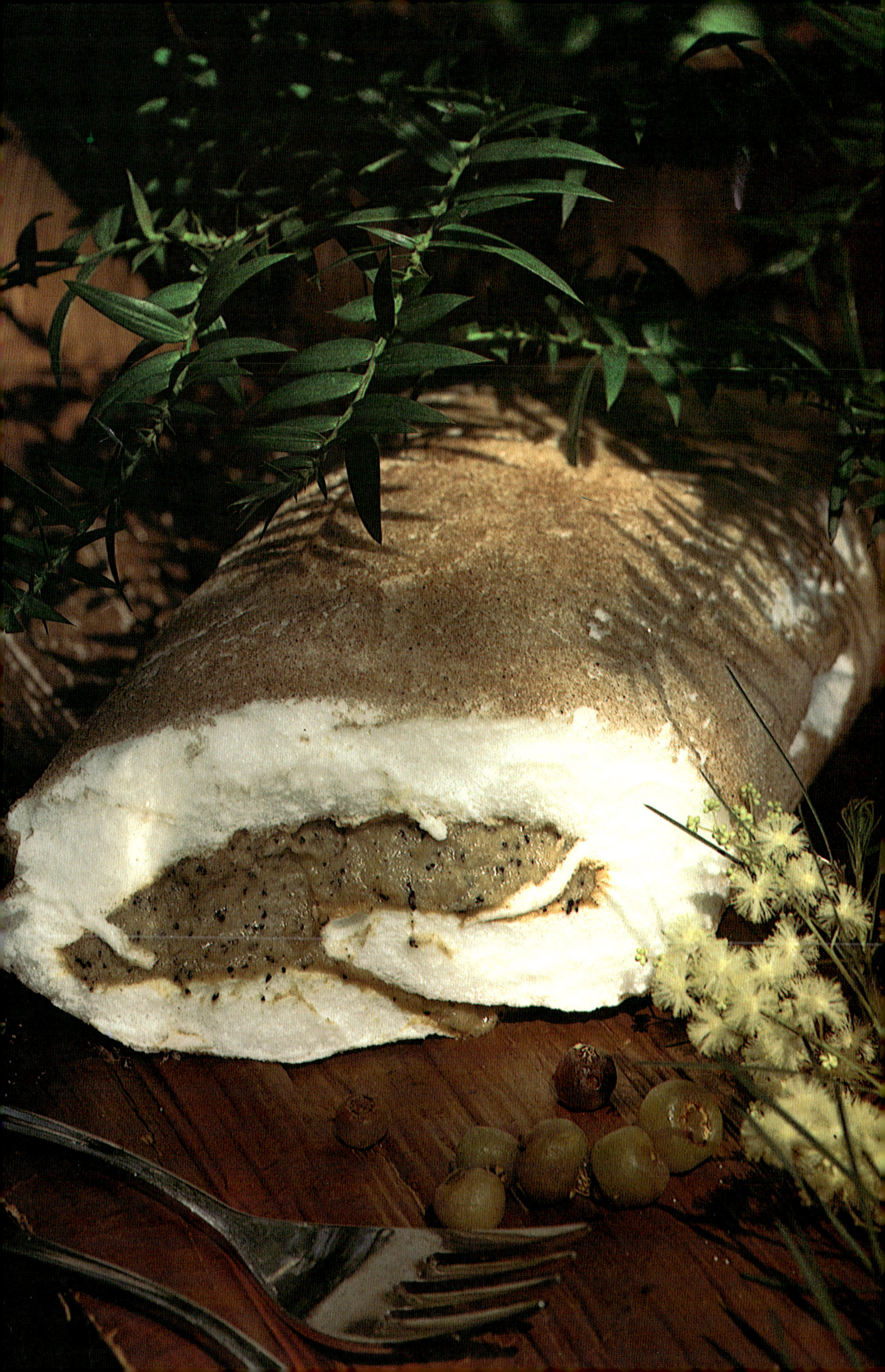

Uniquely Australian

Wild rosella mousse cake

To serve 12

**1 day old sponge, trimmed to 20cm diameter round
2 cups blended rosella flowers
2 cups cream
6 level teaspoons gelatine
¼ cup water
8 egg yolks
1 cup sugar
¼ cup rum diluted with ¼ cup water
rosella flowers for garnish
chocolate curls and whipped cream for garnish**

Cream the egg yolks and sugar. Warm the blended rosella and add it to the creamed egg mixture. In a double boiler cook this mixture until it thickens. Do not allow the mix to boil. Combine gelatine and cold water and dissolve it into the thickened rosella mix. Allow to cool but not to setting temperature. Whip the cream until soft peaks form and fold it into the cooled rosella. Cut the sponge in half and sprinkle both halves with diluted rum. Take a 23cm spring form cake tin and coat the bottom with ⅓ of the rosella mixture. Place in one sponge half and cover it with another ⅓ of the rosella mix. Place the other sponge half on top, finish with the remaining mixture and refrigerate overnight to set. To remove the mousse from the tin, wrap a teatowel soaked in boiling water around the outside of the tin. Release the spring on the tin carefully. Decorate with whipped cream, chocolate curls and rosella flowers.

Rosellas are the modified petals and sepals of fertilised flowers of the introduced weed, Hibiscus sabdariffa. The native hibiscus species do not form an acid crisp fruit. However, it is possible to use the white or yellow flowers of native hibiscus to make a jelly or to pick them and set the petals (without the green sepals) in a clear jelly.

Uniquely Australian

A dessert to ignite the appetite.

Uniquely Australian

Munthari muffins

To make 12 muffins

1½ cups bran
1¼ cups milk
1 egg
¼ cup oil
½ cup caster sugar
1¼ cups self raising flour
1 cup munthari berries

Soak the bran in milk for 5 minutes. Add the beaten egg and oil.
Stir in the sugar and sifted flour. Fold in the munthari berries.
Pour the mix into a greased muffin tray and bake at 190°C for 25 minutes.

Burnt caramel sauce with sugarbag

75g sugar
25g brown sugar
250ml thickened cream
25g sugarbag

Heat the sugars in a pan until browned. Add the cream and reduce to thicken.
Allow to cool. To finish, drizzle the burnt caramel sauce over the muffins.
Serve the sugarbag over the cooled sauce or to the side.

Uniquely Australian

Using blended munthari berries and apple juice as a sweetener to replace some or all of the milk and sugar can heighten the flavour of the berries.

Wattle cones with macadamia nut ice cream

To serve 8

Wattle cones

60g very soft butter
2½ tablespoons (60g) warm honey
⅔ cup (80g) plain flour
½ cup (80g) icing sugar
2 egg whites
1 tablespoon wattle, boiled in 50ml water

Mix the butter and honey. Sieve in the flour and sugar. Mix until smooth. Work in the egg whites and softened wattle. With a palette knife, spread the mix thinly into a 10cm disc on a greased baking tray. Bake at 190°C for 5 to 10 minutes until golden brown. While still hot and pliable, lift from the sheet and form a cone. Stand each cone in a glass to cool.

Macadamia nut ice cream

200g macadamia nuts
375ml milk
375ml cream
5 egg yolks
⅔ cup (150g) sugar

Roast the macadamia nuts lightly. Blend to a fine crumb in a food processor. Bring the milk and nuts to the boil. Mix the yolks and sugar well and slowly pour into the milk while whisking quickly. Keep stirring over a water bath until it thickens. Remove from heat and stir in the cream. Allow to cool then churn in an ice cream machine. Garnish with stewed quandongs and candied wild lime zest.

This recipe combines the first commercial native species, the macadamia, with the second significant product which is wattle. The quandong used as a garnish has the potential to follow suit. However, the production of quandong in plantation as promoted by the CSIRO is doomed to failure since monoculture of this native fruit necessitates the expensive application of undesirable pesticides and removes the wild or native quality as well as its market appeal.

These wattle cones are an excellent accompaniment to any bush ice-cream or they can be served with wild flavoured custards as well.

Quandong pie with lemon aspen ice cream

To serve 6 to 8

Quandong pie

shortcrust pastry
2 cups (200g) dried quandong
1200ml water
1 cup (250g) sugar
¼ cup (35g) arrowroot or potato flour

Simmer the quandongs, water and sugar for 10 minutes. Remove the fruit and thicken the syrup with the starch mixed with a little water. Return the fruit to the sauce and set aside to cool. Line a pie tin with shortcrust pastry, fill with the quandong mixture and top with a pastry lid.
Bake at 190°C for 45 minutes.

Lemon aspen ice cream

100g lemon aspen
250g sugar
125ml water
6 egg yolks
500ml milk
500ml cream
100g glucose

Simmer the lemon aspen and sugar in the water for 5 minutes. Whisk the yolks and the milk together. Pour in the lemon aspen mixture. Cook over a boiling water bath while stirring constantly until the mixture thickens.
Remove from the heat. Stir in the cream and glucose.
Strain through a fine sieve. Chill and churn.

Uniquely Australian

Quandong pie is a traditional dessert using this popular desert fruit. Apricots compliment the flavour of quandongs very well as can be put to good use as an extender. A touch of orange liqueur also enhances the taste.

Uniquely Australian

Black apple flan

To serve 4

Flan

**1 sheet of puff pastry cut to 4 x10cm rounds
4 medium black apples, sliced
icing sugar for dusting**

Custard

**120ml thin vanilla custard
½ teaspoon wattle**

Garnish

**piping chocolate
native fruit ice cream
native mint**

Arrange the black apple slices on the pastry rounds. Bake at 220°C for 10 minutes or until the pastry is cooked. Dust with icing sugar and glaze with a flame burner or under the griller. Bring the custard and wattle to the boil and allow to cool. Decorate the serving plate with piped chocolate outlines of gum tree leaves and fill these leaves with the wattle custard.

Plate the black apple flans, some ice cream and the garnish with native mint. Serve with extra custard or whipped cream on the side.

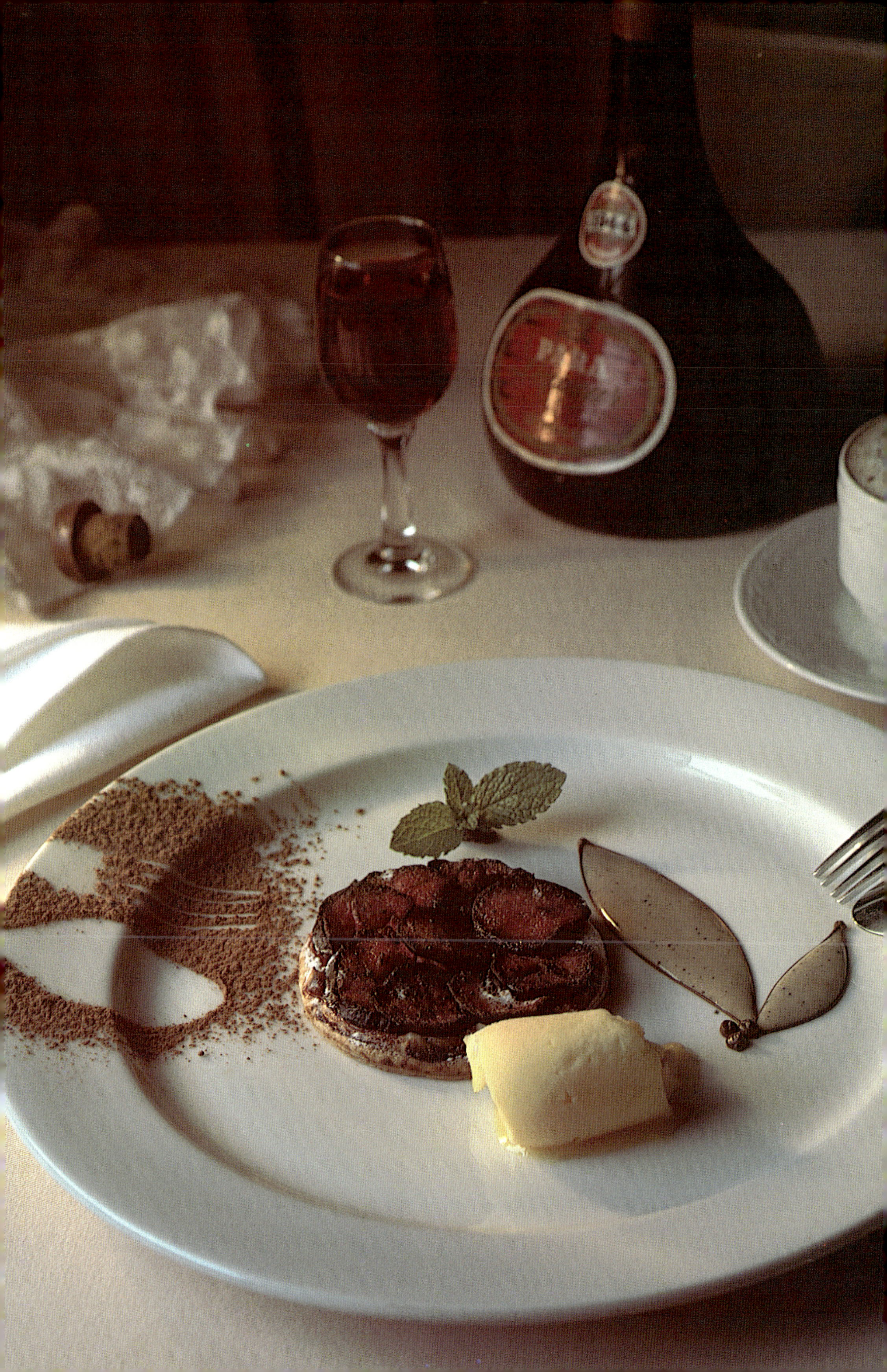

Bunya nut torte 1.

To serve 8 to 10

200g unsalted butter
¾ cup (200g) sugar
10 egg yolks
150g raw bunya bunya nut meal
100g hazelnut meal
2 tablespoons (10g) breadbrumbs
10 egg whites
a pinch of salt
¼ cup (60g) castor sugar

Cream the butter and sugar until light and fluffy. Slowly add the beaten egg yolks a small amount at a time to avoid curdling the creamed butter. Shell the bunya nuts by squashing them with a mallet and mince or blend the nut meat to a meal. Fold the nut meals and the breadcrumbs into the butter mixture. Whisk the egg whites with a pinch of salt until peaks form. Slowly add the castor sugar and beat until the whites are stiff and glossy. Whisk ⅓ of the whites into the bunya nut mixture and very gently fold in the remainder. Do not over-mix. Pour into a 23cm greased spring form tin and bake in a moderate oven (about 180°C) for 1½ hours or until cooked through. Cool to room temperature and slice into 3 equal rounds. Brush each round with a honey and water solution.

Bunya nut cream

500ml cream
500g bunya bunya nuts, boiled and shelled
1½ tablespoons gelatine
½ cup boiling water

Reserve some of the prepared and halved bunya nuts for decoration. Blend the remaining cooked nuts in a food processor adding a little of the cream to make a smooth paste. Some diluted honey can be added as sweetener and to assist the blending. Whip the remaining cream until stiff and combine with the bunya nut paste. Soak the gelatine leaves in a small volume of cold water until soft. Add the boiling water, dissolve the gelatine and leave to cool. Fold into the bunya nut cream and leave to stand for 1 hour. This will give the cream a firmer, mousse-style texture which is strong enough to hold the torte together. Fill and layer the torte with the cream and mask the sides and the top with cream as well.
Dip each of the reserved bunya nut halves partly into melted chocolate.
Place onto greaseproof paper to set. Decorate the torte to finish.

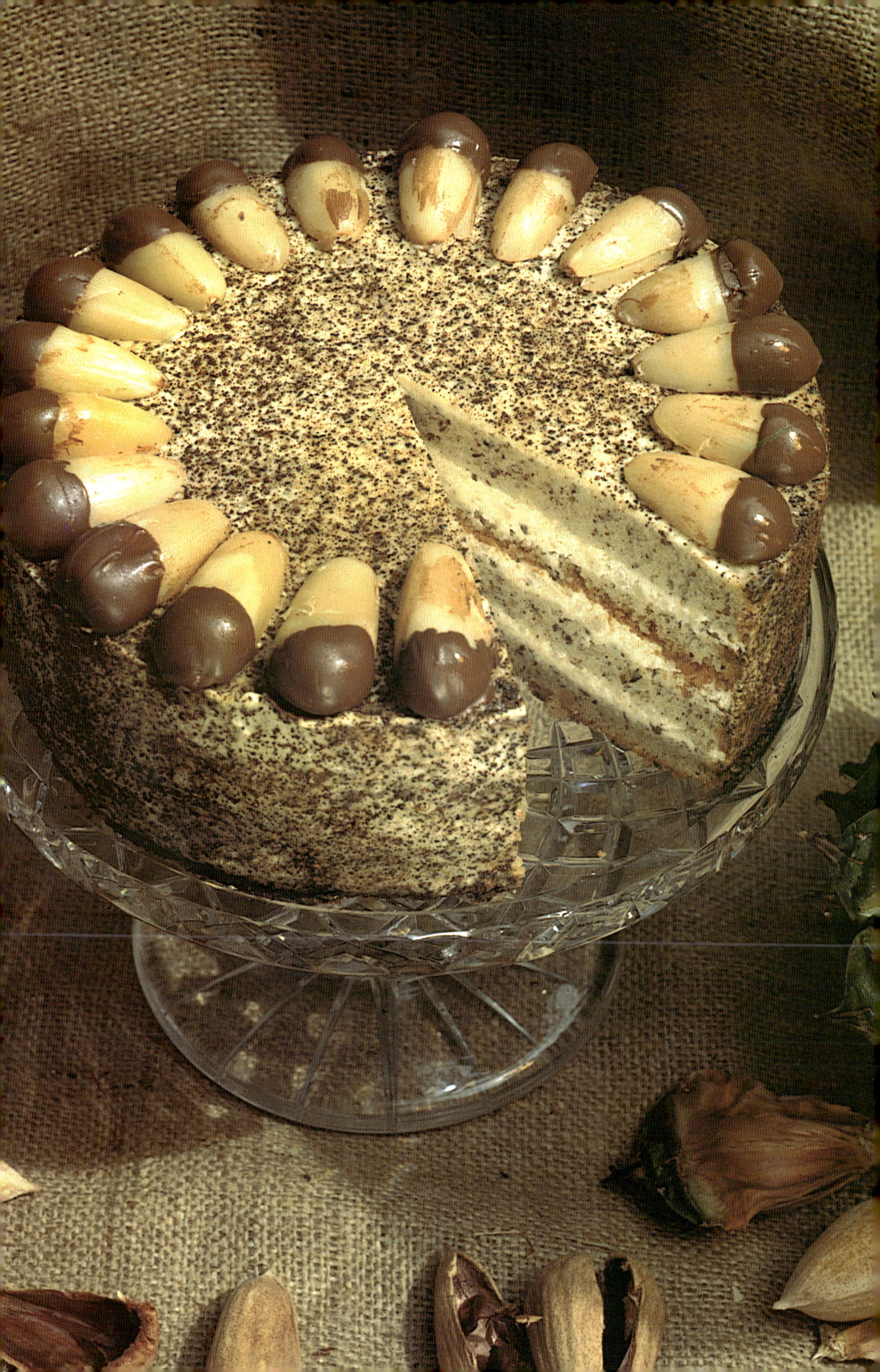

Bunya nut torte 2.

This recipe is a low refined sugar and low fat variation of the preceding torte. The first is ideal for those special occasions while this one can be a more common indulgence.

Cake mix

100g bunya nuts, boiled and shelled
100g hazelnut meal
2 cups soy milk
½ cup maple syrup
1 teaspoon pure vanilla essence
4 egg whites
½ teaspoon cream of tartar
2 cups well-squeezed ricotta cheese

Blend the nuts with the soy milk until smooth and creamy. Add the remaining soy milk, the maple syrup, vanilla and cardamom. Beat the egg whites and cream of tartar to soft peaks and very gently fold into the nut mixture. Spoon the mixture into a 20cm greased spring form cake tin and bake at 180°C for 90 minutes. Allow to cool before removing from the spring form tin.

Frosting

3 tablespoons water chestnut starch
1 cup clear, unsweetened apple juice
2 tablespoons apple concentrate
½ cup maple syrup
2 teaspoons pure vanilla essence
500g well squeezed ricotta cheese

Make a paste from the starch and some of the juice. Add the remaining juice and the concentrate and bring to the boil, stirring until thick. Cool and then add the sweetener and the vanilla. In a food processor, cream this mixture with the ricotta cheese and decorate the cake as for the preceding recipe.

The term, bunya bunya, is from the Yagara language which was spoken by Aborigines who lived in and around what is now the city of Brisbane.

Uniquely Australian

Illawarra plum cheesecake and rosella sauce

To serve 8

Crust

**30 bunya nuts, boiled and shelled
1½ cups macadamia nuts**

Blend the nuts to a fine crumb. Press into a greased pie plate and bake in a moderate oven for 25 minutes or until brown.

Filling

**1 cup Illawarra plum fruits
1½ cups low fat ricotta cheese
3 tablespoons apple juice concentrate
1 tablespoon lemon aspen juice
¾ cup apple juice
6 teaspoons gelatine
3 egg whites
a pinch of cream of tartar**

Blend the plums, ricotta cheese, apple concentrate and lemon aspen juice until smooth. Soak the gelatine in the apple juice and warm the mixture to dissolve the gelatine. Add it to the plum mixture. Beat the egg whites briefly then add the cream of tartar and continue beating until stiff. Fold into the plum mixture. Pour into the prepared pie crust and refrigerate.

Rosella sauce

**rosella flowers
maple syrup**

Blend a handful of rosellas with maple syrup to taste. Add water if necessary.

Uniquely Australian

Bunya nut ice cream with sugarbag

To serve 4 to 6

20 bunya nuts, boiled and shelled
2 cups soy milk
½ cup maple syrup
2 teaspoons gelatine
2 teaspoons (10ml) sugarbag

While the shelled nuts are still hot from boiling blend them in a food processor. Add the soy milk slowly until the blended nuts have a custard consistency. Sweeten with the maple syrup. Soak the gelatine in a small volume of cold water and then warm it to dissolve completely. Add this to the bunya nut mixture and place it into the freezer for an hour. Beat the mix with an electric beater for 10 minutes. Refreeze and repeat after another hour. Alternatively, chill the mix and churn it in an ice cream machine.

Serve the ice cream drizzled with sugarbag and with a garnish of wild fruits to contrast the sweetness with a little acidity from the fruit.

Recent research suggests that bushfoods like the bunya bunya nut are more filling than equivalent cultivated foods with the same amount of starch. The reason may lie in the quality of the complex carbohydrates in bushfoods and the rate at which they are absorbed. This makes bushfoods which are high in these starches the ideal slimmers' foods.

Uniquely Australian

The maple syrup in this recipe may one day be replaced with collected sap from Eucalyptus gunnii which is found in Tasmania and southern Victoria. Other eucalypts and perhaps some of the desert wattles or the desert oak, all of which exude sweet gum, could also be potential sources of natural sweeteners.

Nyngan mud cake

200g unsweetened chocolate
¾ cup butter
2 heaped tablespoons wattle
1½ cups water
2 eggs
2½ teaspoons baking soda
½ cup rum
1 cup self-raising flour
1 cup plain cake flour
1½ cups honey

Heat the chocolate, butter, wattle and water until the chocolate and butter are melted. Stir well to blend the mixture to smoothness. Allow to cool for about 10 minutes. In a separate saucepan, heat the rum and light the vapour to burn off harsh chemical esters and make the rum taste smoother. Extinguish the flame by covering the saucepan with a well-fitting lid. Add the rum to the wattle mixture then add in the eggs while stirring. Sift the remaining dry ingredients into a bowl and then sift them again into the combined mixture. Fold in until the mixture is smooth. Divide between two greased 20cm cake tins and bake at 180°C for 30 minutes then reduce the heat to 150°C for another 45 minutes or until cooked. Finish with wattle sauce (see page 130) and a whipped cream filling.

This recipe is based on the American Mississippi mud cake and is made Australian by the rum and wattle. However, this recipe is named after the NSW town of Nyngan which is an Aboriginal word meaning spreading waters or wide lake. The regular flooding of the Bogon River spreads alluvial muds over the surrounding flatlands and as the waters recede the profusion of bushfoods provided a feast for the local people. These days, the effects of the flooding are exacerbated by inappropriate land use by both farmers and townies.

Uniquely Australian

Lemon myrtle bavarois

10 lemon myrtle leaves
450ml milk
5 egg yolks
¾ cup sugar
2 teaspoons (15g) gelatine
¼ cup warm water
400ml cream

Shred the lemon myrtle leaves and bring them to the boil in the milk. Stir in the sugar and dissolve it then leave the mixture to cool for 5 to 10 minutes. Whip the cream. Over boiling water, strain the milk onto the egg yolks while whisking continuously until it thickens. Soak the gelatine in the water and add it to the egg mixture. Transfer the container onto ice and continue to whisk the mixture until it thickens further. Quickly fold in the whipped cream. Pour into oiled molds. Top with a rosella jelly and allow to set in the refrigerator. Turn the bavarois out of their molds and onto a serving plate. Garnish with a fresh lemon myrtle leaf.

Try this recipe substituting native aniseed leaves for the lemon myrtle or boil 1 heaped tablespoon of wattle in the milk and strain it to make a wattle bavarois.
Try maple syrup as a substitute sweetener or add sugarbag to the whipped cream and use ¼ cup of fructose instead of the given quantity of sucrose.

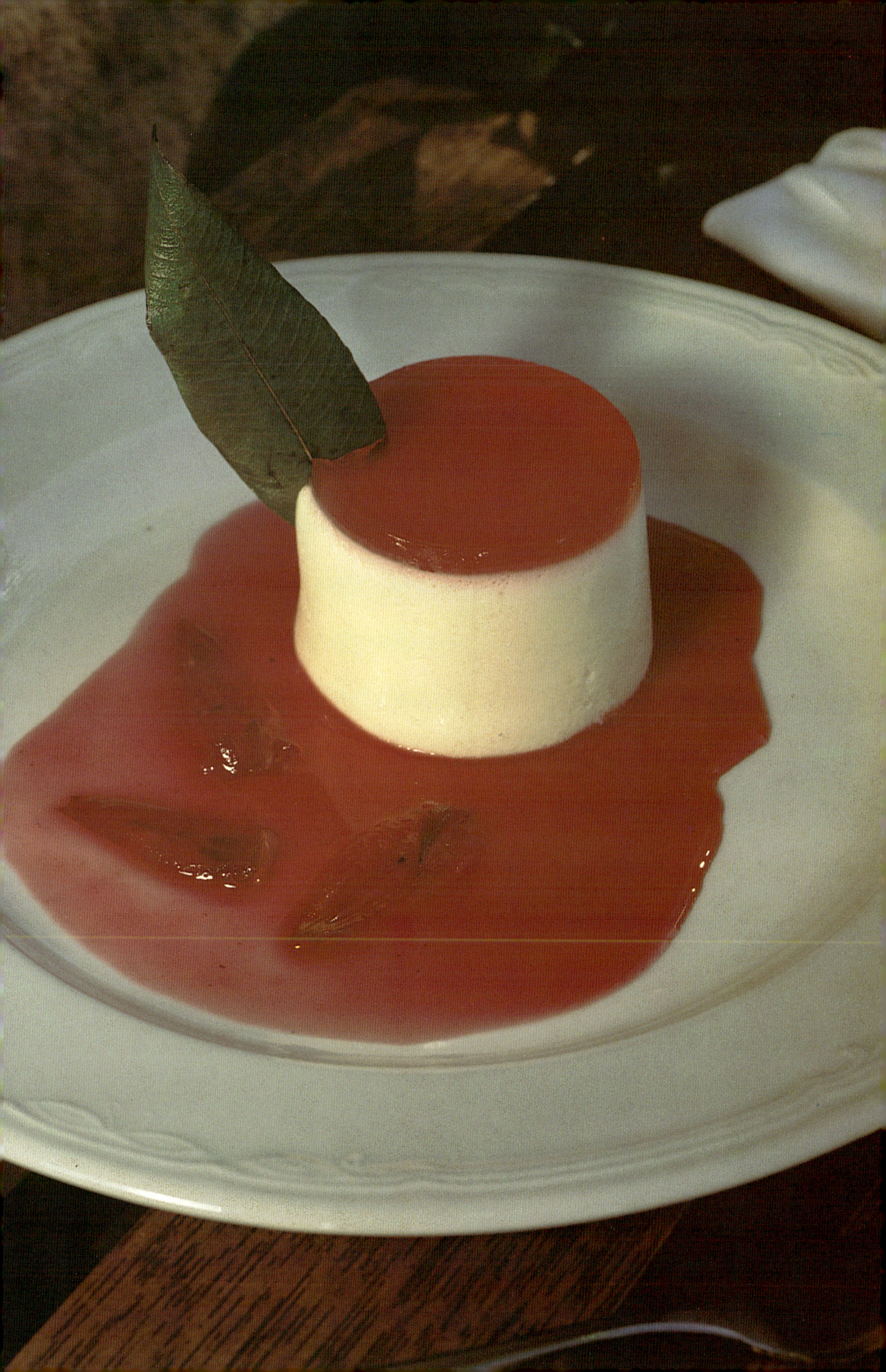

Wattle pancakes with lemon aspen curd

To serve 2

3 cups pancake batter
2 teaspoons wattle
½ cup water
oil for frying

Bring the wattle to the boil and leave it to cool down a little. Mix the wattle into the batter and fry the pancakes. Try wattle sour dough pancakes using batter that has been left to ferment for several days.

Fill the prepared pancakes with whipped cream or bunya nut cream (see page 134). Finish each pancake with a topping of lemon aspen curd.

Lemon aspen curd

Makes 2 cups

4 eggs, beaten
1 cup sugar or 1½ cups juice concentrate
¼ cup lemon aspen juice
60g butter, chopped

Combine all the ingredients in a double boiler and stir constantly as the mixture comes to the boil. Simmer until thick and the curd coats the back of the spoon. Pour into sterilised jars, cap with sterilised lids and cool. Store in the refrigerator.

This curd can be made quickly in the microwave:
Heat the combined ingredients in a bowl on high power,
stirring every 30 seconds until thick.

For most recipes requiring wattle, use the spent grounds left from brewing a wattle drink. Store leftover grounds frozen for later use.

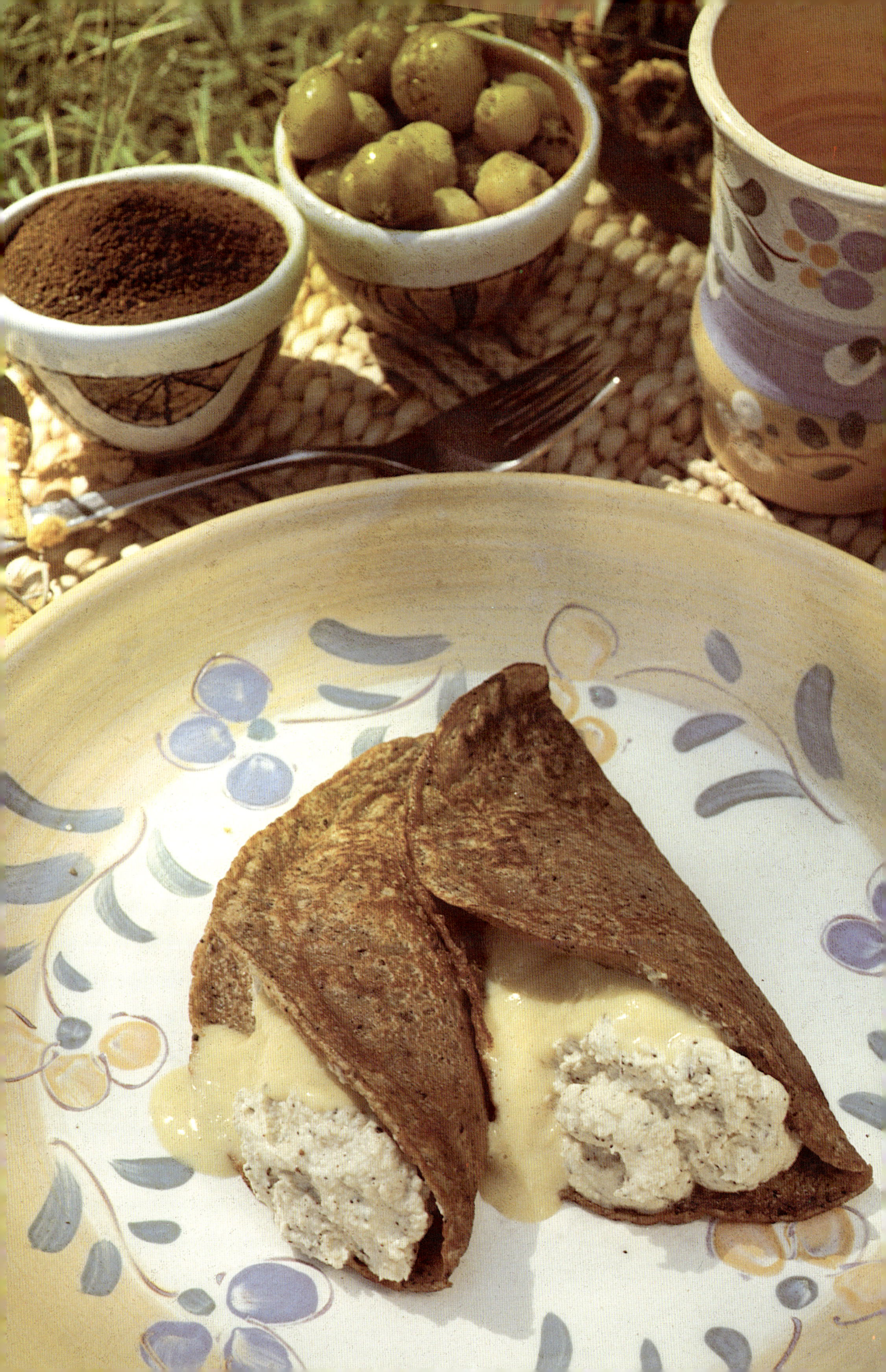

Uniquely Australian

Illawarra plum and riberry tart

To serve 8

Pastry

1⅔ cups plain flour
⅓ cup castor sugar
100g softened butter
2 eggs

Combine the dry ingredients and quickly beat the softened butter through the mix. Add the eggs one at a time, being careful not to over-beat the mix. If the pastry is over-worked it will become tough and lose that delicious 'shortness' of good sweet pastry. Wrap the dough in plastic wrap and refrigerate for at least an hour. On a well-floured bench, quickly roll out the pastry to about 5mm thickness and shape to fit a 20cm flan tin. Press the pastry up to the sides of the tin. Rest the prepared case in the refrigerator for at least 20 minutes.

Macadamia nut cream

300g butter
1 cup icing sugar
5 egg yolks
150g macadamia nuts, finely crushed
2 tablespoons arrowroot or cornflour

Cream the butter and sugar until light and creamy. Add the yolks, slowly beating in one at a time and then quickly beat in the macadamia meal and arrowroot. Pour into the pastry case.

To finish

1½ cups, cored and frozen
⅔ cup riberries, frozen

Scatter the frozen fruits over the macadamia nut cream and bake in a pre-heated oven at 180°C for 50 minutes. Leaving the fruits frozen reduces their drying during the baking. The tart is ready once a skewer comes out clean even though the centre of the tart may still look uncooked. This will firm on cooling. When the tart is cool, prepare a glaze as follows: Place 2 tablespoons of Kakadu plum jelly (or alternatively, an apricot conserve) in a heavy saucepan with 1 tablespoonful of water. Bring to a brisk boil and lightly brush over the tart. This tart is delicious cold but is at its best served warm with cream or ice cream.

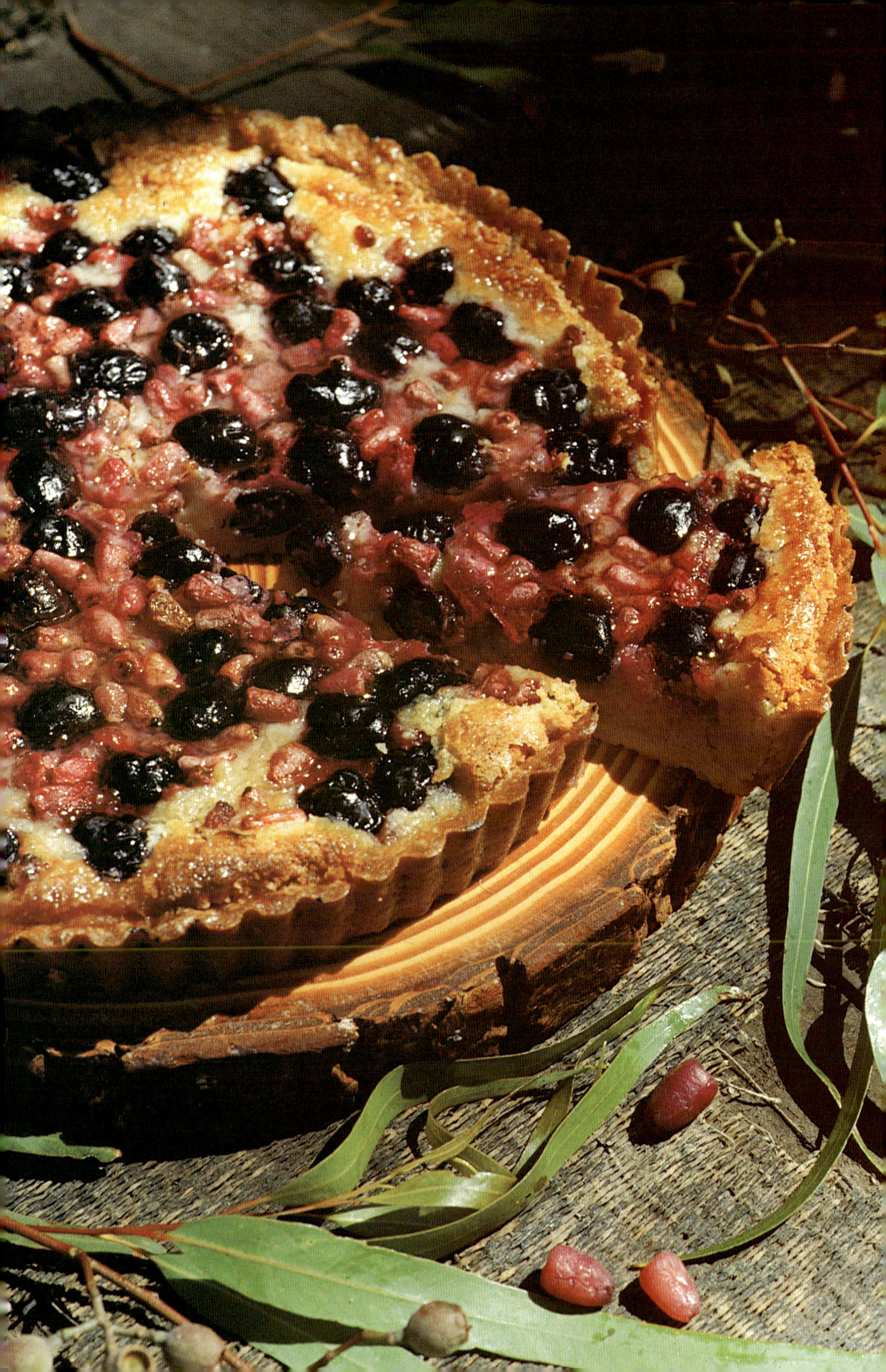

Uniquely Australian

Lemon aspen curd tartlets

Line small tartlet shells with sweet crust pastry (see preceding recipe). Bake for 20 to 25 minutes in a moderate oven until golden brown.

To make 12 tartlets

Lemon aspen curd

**100g lemon aspen
juice from 6 lemons
6 whole eggs
9 egg yolks
1½ cups sugar
¼ cup of milk
400g unsalted butter**

Blend the lemon aspen fruits and lemon juice together. Combine this juice with all the other ingredients in a heavy bottomed (non-aluminium) saucepan. The liquid will appear curdled at this stage but this will disappear on cooking. Heat gently, stirring constantly with a wooden spoon until the butter melts and the sugar dissolves completely. Turn the heat up to medium and continue stirring until the mixture thickens and coats the back of the spoon. This must be judged carefully as if the heating is too prolonged or too hot the mixture will curdle and separate. The curd should be a homogeneous yellow colour and have a silken texture. When the curd is cooked to this stage remove from heat and strain through a fine strainer into a clean bowl. Leave to cool and then spoon it into the prepared sweet pastry shells.

An idea for using the left-overs from straining the curd is to make a shortbread or incorporate it into the sweet crust pastry recipe used here.

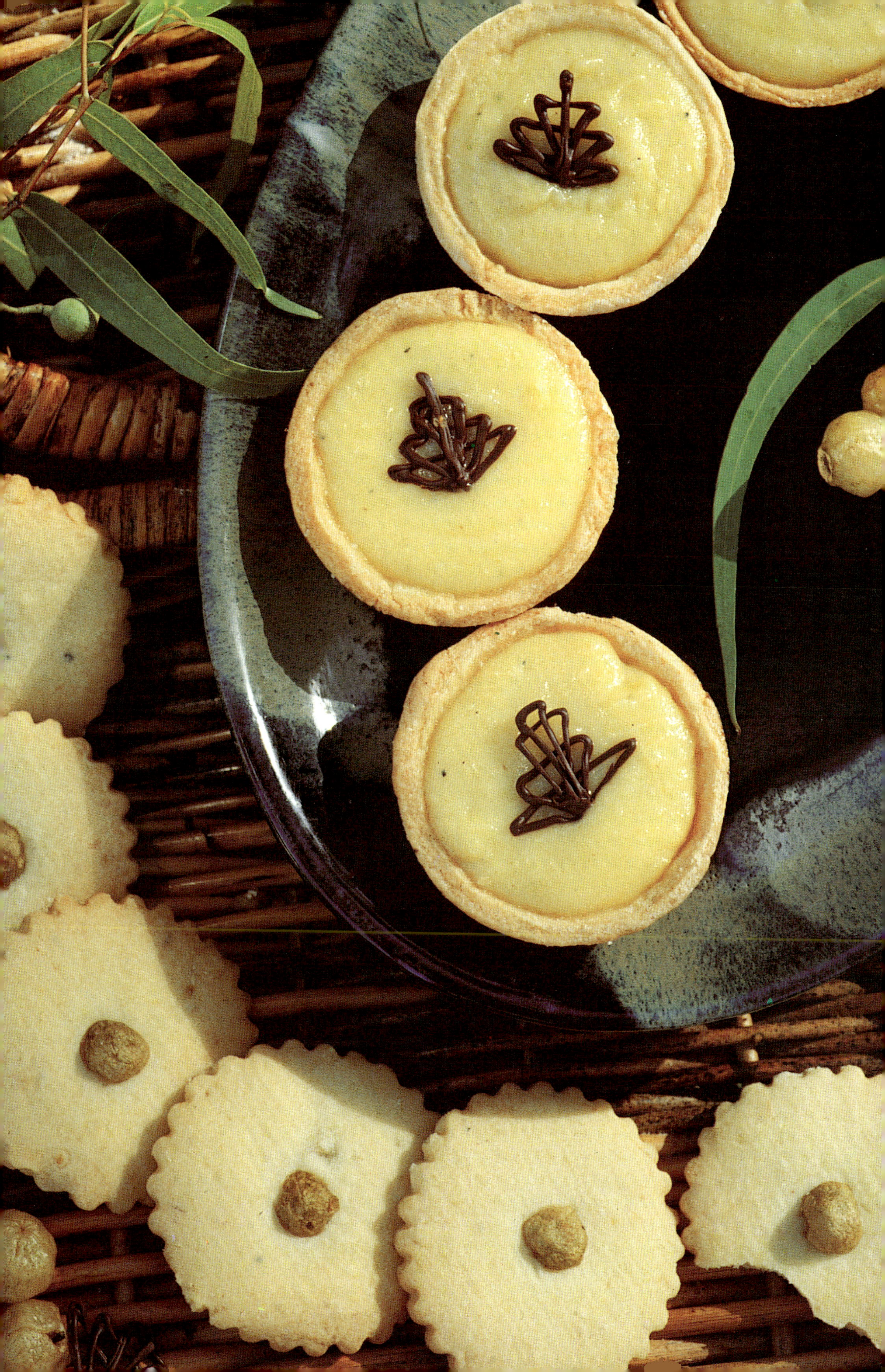

Uniquely Australian

Wild rosella and native currant tartlets

Makes 6 tartlets

Base

**1 cup macadamia nuts
1 cup walnuts or almonds
1 cup rolled oats
pear juice**

Blend the rolled oats and nuts, then add a little pear juice to form a firm pastry. Press into oiled tartlet shells and bake at 180°C for 30 minutes or until lightly browned.

Filling 1

**1 cup wild rosella flowers
2 cups pear purée (use fresh blanched pears or canned pears in natural juice)
2 tablespoons honey (or to taste)
2 heaped tablespoons kuzu or arrowroot**

Combine the rosella, pear purée and honey in a saucepan and boil for 15 to 20 minutes. Dilute the kuzu in a little water and mix into the boiling rosella sauce. Continue to heat and stir until the fruit mixture becomes thick and clear (2 to 3 minutes).

Filling 2

**1 cup native currants
2 cups of pear purée
3 tablespoons of honey
2 heaped tablespoons kuzu or arrowroot**

As for the preceding filling. The native currant filling can be strained if desired, to remove the tiny seeds of the currants.

Pour the rosella filling into the pastry shells simultaneously with a dairy or soy milk custard to form the swirling pattern. Allow to cool and refrigerate before serving. Repeat with the second filling and custard to make the native currant tartlets.

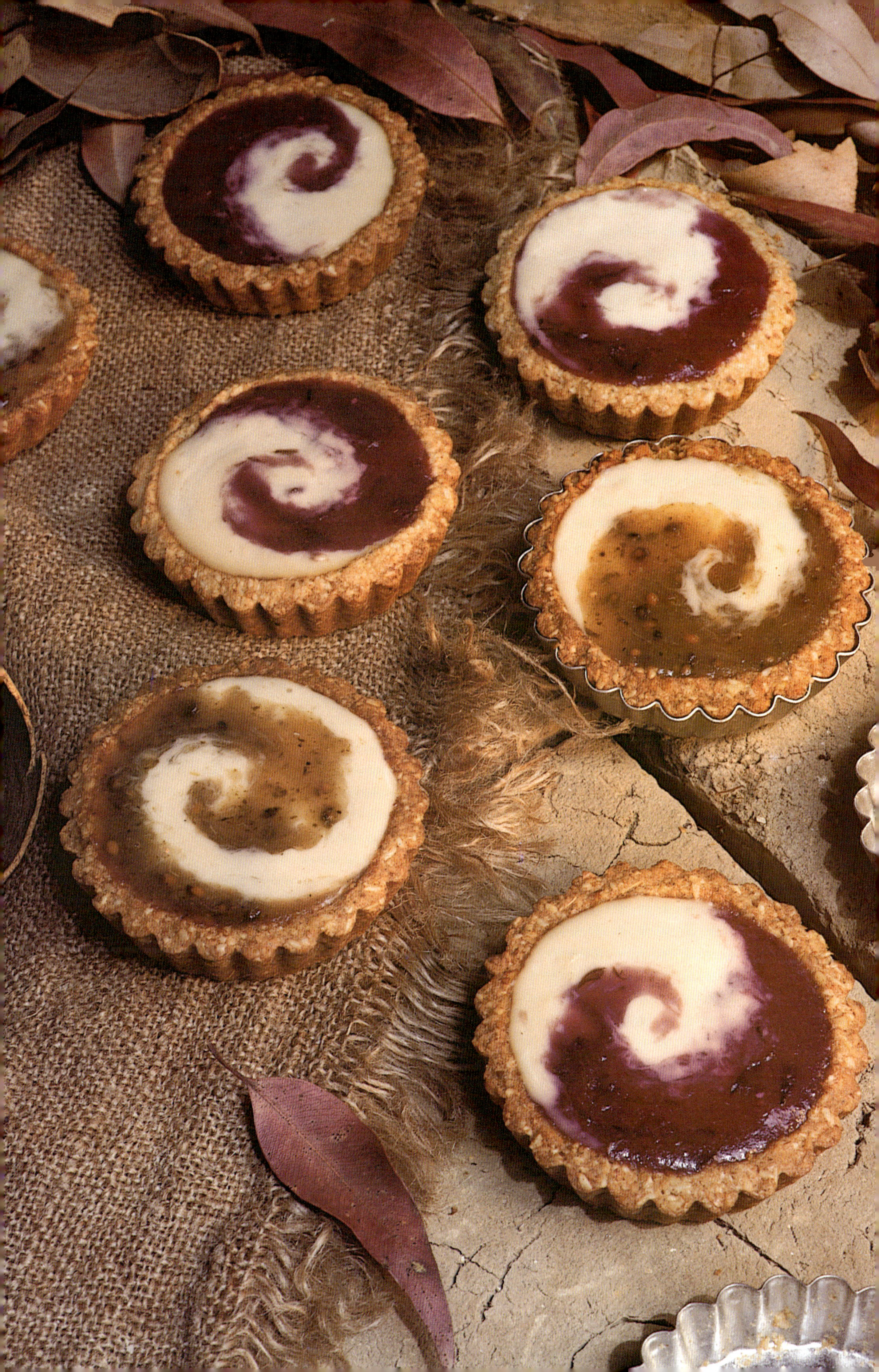

Bushfood breads

Basic recipe

30g compressed baker's yeast
400ml warm water
200ml warm skim milk
2½ cups unbleached white flour
2½ cups wholemeal flour
extra flour

Additions

1 cup finely chopped or flaked macadamia nuts
1 cup of rainforest honey
1 teaspoon milled leaves of lemon myrtle or native aniseed *or*

1 cup fresh seedless riberry fruits
1 cup of bush honey
½ teaspoon cinnamon *or*

1 tablespoon wattle boiled in ½ cup water and cooled
½ cup golden syrup or maple syrup
2 bananas, chopped or mashed.

Combine the yeast with the liquids and stir to disperse the yeast. Add any sweetener or if using wattle, stir the wattle slurry into the yeast mixture at this stage. Sift the flours into a large bowl and add back the bran. Add any dry ingredients to be used as flavourings and mix through. Make a well in the flour and pour in the yeast mixture. Chop the yeast into the flour using a spatula and mix until homogenous. The mixture will be quite wet and sticky. Cover the bowl with a towel and leave the mix in a warm place for an hour to rise. Sprinkle the top liberally with flour and turn the dough out onto a floured bench. Knead the bread very gently for only 30 seconds or so to release the fermentation gases and reduce the tackiness. Shape into a loaf in a well-buttered bread tin lined on the base with baking paper. Bake at 180°C for 30 to 40 minutes. Leave to cool for 10 minutes and remove from the tin.

Serve with lemon aspen curd, eucalyptus butter or any proprietary preserve, for example, Kakadu plum jelly (pictured) or wild rosella jam (bottled). Eucalyptus butter is made by stirring food grade eucalyptus oil dropwise into softened butter.

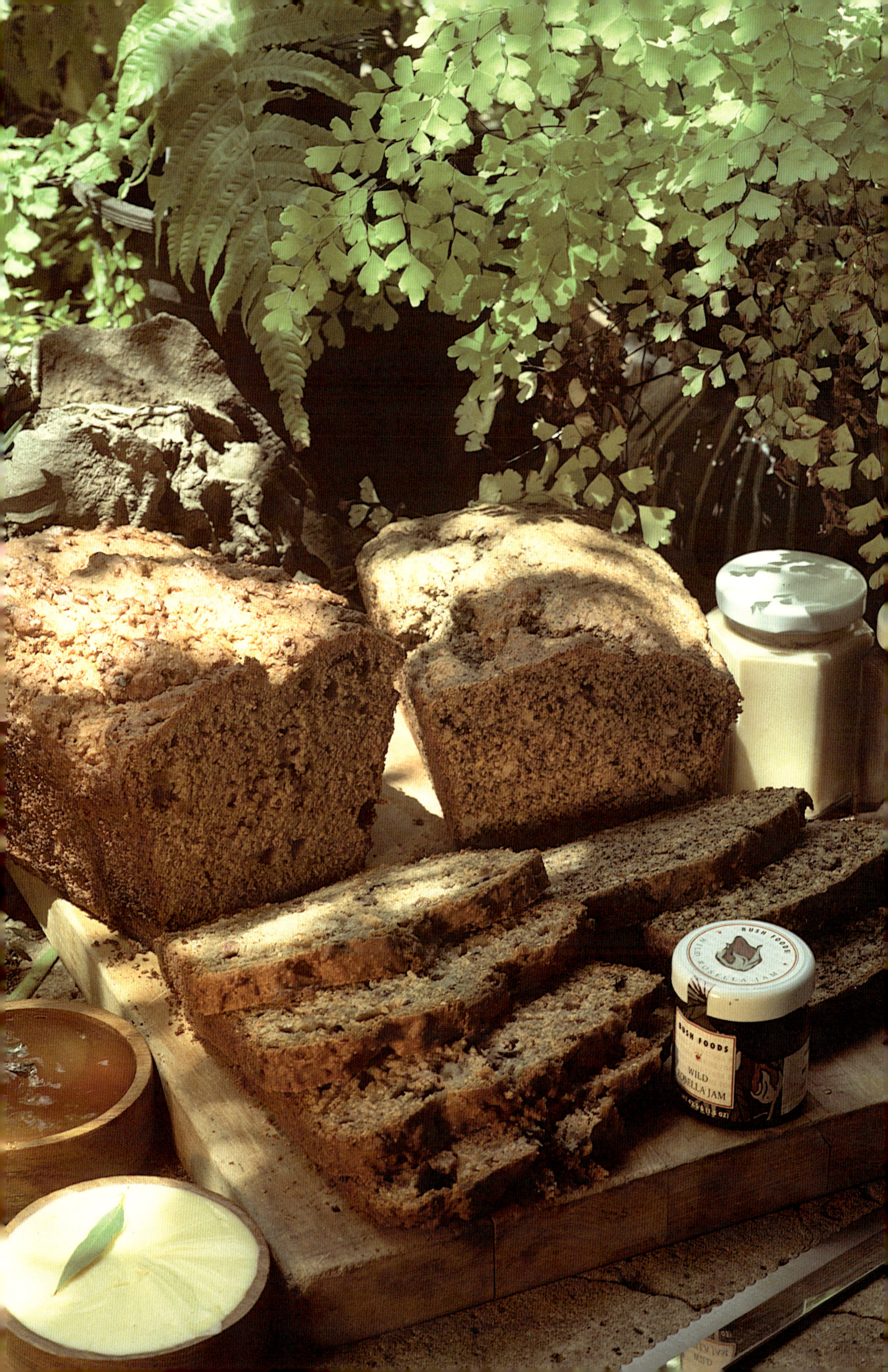
BUSH FOODS
WILD ROSELLA JAM
BUSH FOODS
WILD
ROSELLA JAM

Uniquely Australian

Riberry muffins

To make 24 muffins

4 cups unbleached white flour
1 teaspoon bicarbonate of soda
½ cup macadamia nut oil
1 egg yolk
1½ cups apple juice
1 cup native flower honey
½ tablespoon pure vanilla essence
2½ cups (300g) riberries

Sift soda with flour in a large mixing bowl. Blend liquid ingredients until completely smooth and pour onto flour mix. Beat rapidly with a wooden spoon. Add riberries and gently fold in. Spoon into greased muffin trays and place into a pre-heated oven at 180°C. Turn down to 150°C and bake for 30 minutes.

The riberries can be replaced with any of the small berry fruits, for example, midyim, appleberries, munthari or even quandong pieces. Fruits high in acid are less suitable unless pre-soaked in maple or sugar syrup. Try adding slivered macadamia or bunya nuts or an infusion of wattle.

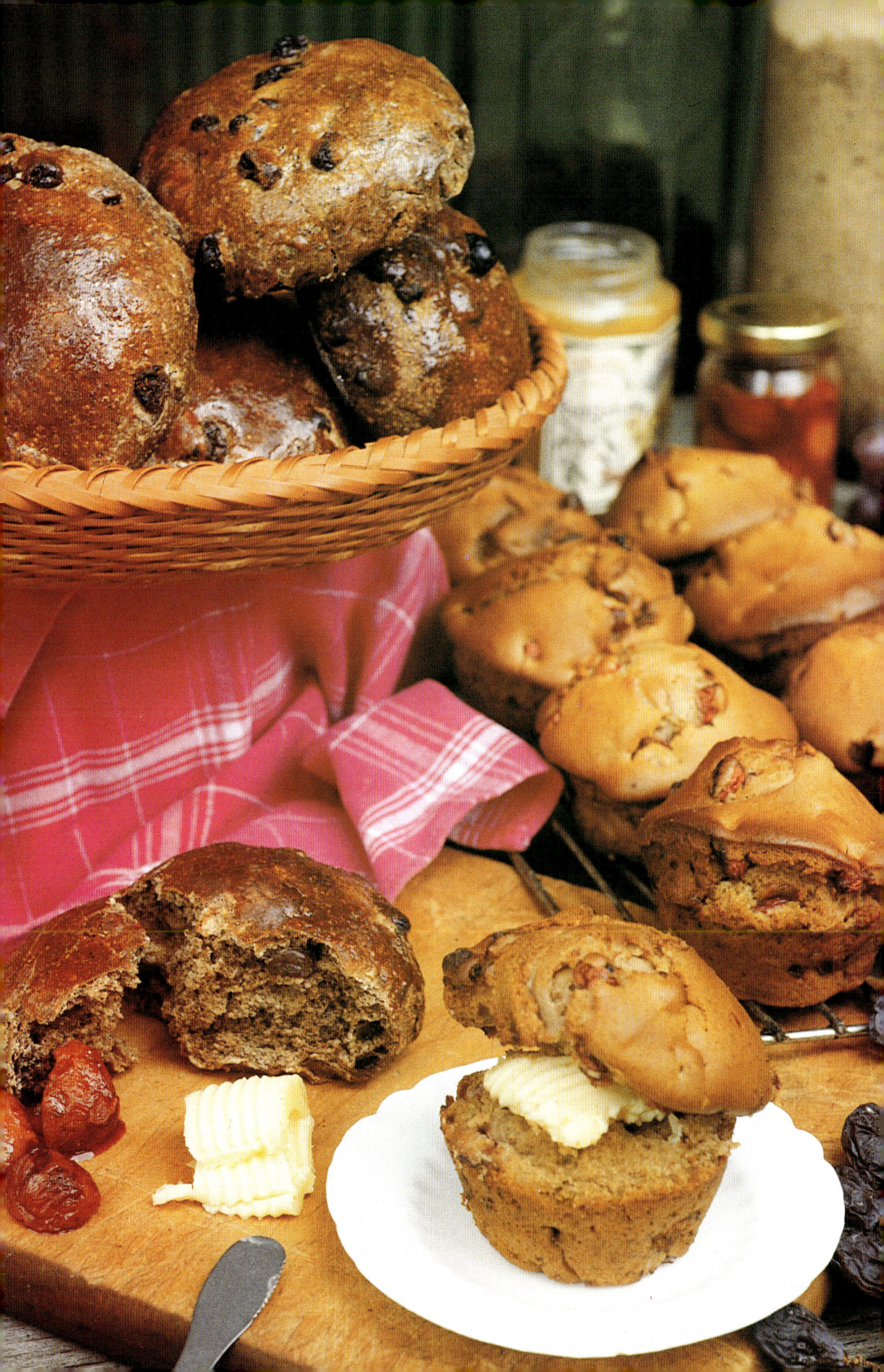

Thumbprint biscuits

1 tablespoon wattle grounds
½ cup maple syrup
½ cup almonds
½ cup macadamia nuts
1 cup rolled oats
1 cup wholemeal flour
½ cup macadamia oil

The wattle grounds used can be left-over from making the beverage or for a stronger wattle flavour use fresh grounds boiled in ¼ cup of water and ½ cup of maple syrup. In separate bowls, mix the dry ingredients together and the wet ingredients together, then combine the mixtures. Shape into biscuits and place on an oiled baking sheet.

Topping

sugarless berry preserve or wild fruit jam
riberries

Make a slight indentation in the centre of each biscuit and spoon in the preserve and riberries. Bake at 180°C for 15 to 20 minutes.

When brewing herb teas or cooking with fragrant fruits like riberries or munthari, it is suggested that the billy or saucepan be covered to retain the full flavour of the essential oils. This way, the oils distil back into the tea. Most herb teas also need to be infused a little longer than conventional tea leaf.

Native herb teas can be made from the leaves of many fragrant plants including lemon myrtle, native aniseed and native sarsparilla (pictured opposite). However, it is important to know the essential oil profile of the leaves used and to avoid any harmful varieties.

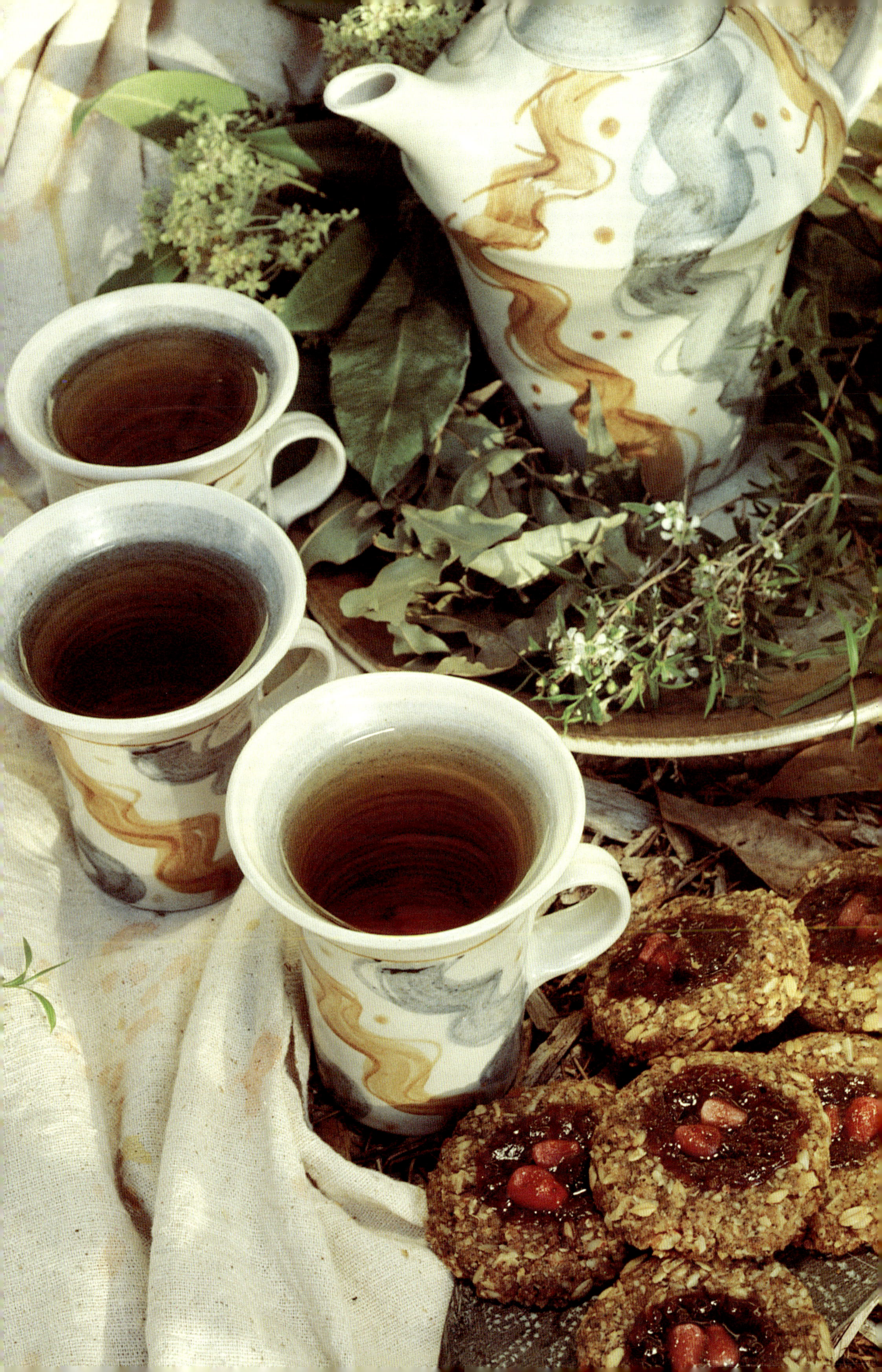

Riberry jelly

1 large banana
2 nectarines
3 cups apple juice
30g agar-agar strips or 2 tablespoons powder
½ cup riberries

Cream

1 cup soy milk
1 tablespoon creamed coconut
1 level tablespoon kuzu or arrowroot
maple syrup to taste
shredded coconut or macadamia nut flakes for garnish

Cut the banana and nectarines and arrange the pieces in a large glass. In a saucepan bring the apple juice and agar-agar to the boil, stirring until the agar-agar dissolves. Remove from the heat and fold in the riberry fruits. Carefully pour over the fruit and refrigerate to set.

Combine the soy milk and creamed coconut and bring to the boil. Sweeten with maple syrup. Make the kuzu into a thin paste with cold water and add it to the boiling liquid. Stir constantly until thick (2 to 3 minutes).

Pour over the set jelly and refrigerate again. Sprinkle with lightly toasted shredded coconut or macadamia nut flakes.

The Tasmanian eucalypt, E. gunnii is being planted out for its production of a maple syrup substitute. Gum syrup could be used instead of maple in all recipes requiring a sweetener and its production in polycultural systems is far more appropriate than clearing our rich tropical rainforests to grow sugar cane in monoculture.

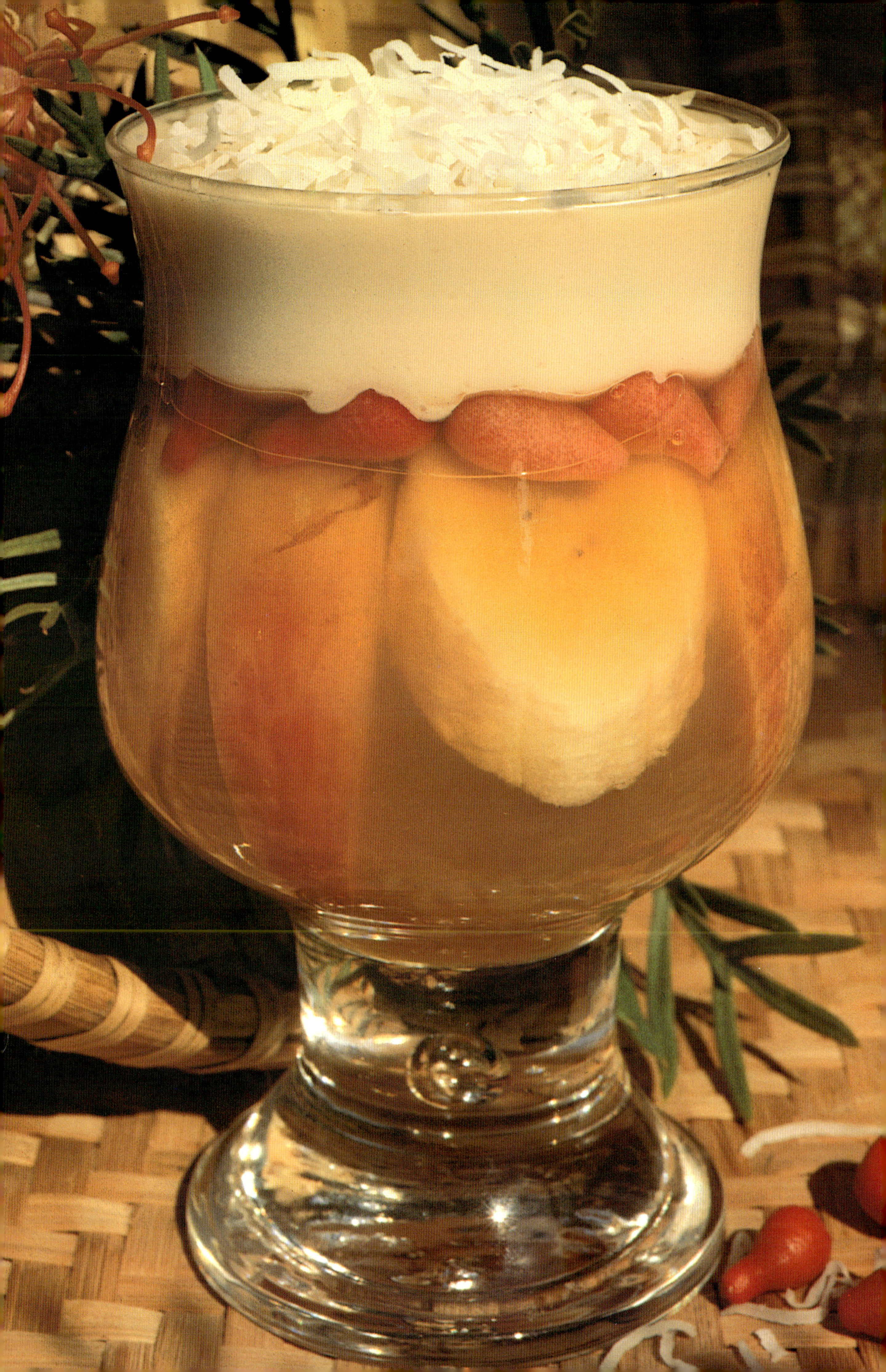

Wattle jelly cups

To make 4 to 6 serves

Wattle concentrate

2 tablespoons wattle
1 cup water

Make a wattle concentrate by boiling the wattle in the water while stirring constantly. Strain and reserve the grounds.

Base

1 cup couscous
2 cups water
maple syrup to taste
2 tablespoons wattle concentrate
2 heaped teaspoons reserved wattle grounds

Combine all the ingredients in a saucepan and cook on medium heat stirring constantly for 15 to 20 minutes or until the couscous is soft and all the water is absorbed. Half-fill the dessert cups or bowls with the mixture and leave to cool.

Jelly

2 cups clear apple juice
½ cup wattle concentrate
2 tablespoons kuzu or arrowroot

Bring the juice and wattle concentrate to the boil. Make a thin paste from the starch in a small amount of cold water or extra juice and add it to the boiling liquid. Stir constantly for 2 to 3 minutes until the jelly thickens.
Pour the jelly on top of the prepared wattle couscous and refrigerate.
Garnish with native mint and serve on its own or
with a sweet soy custard, cream. or ice cream.

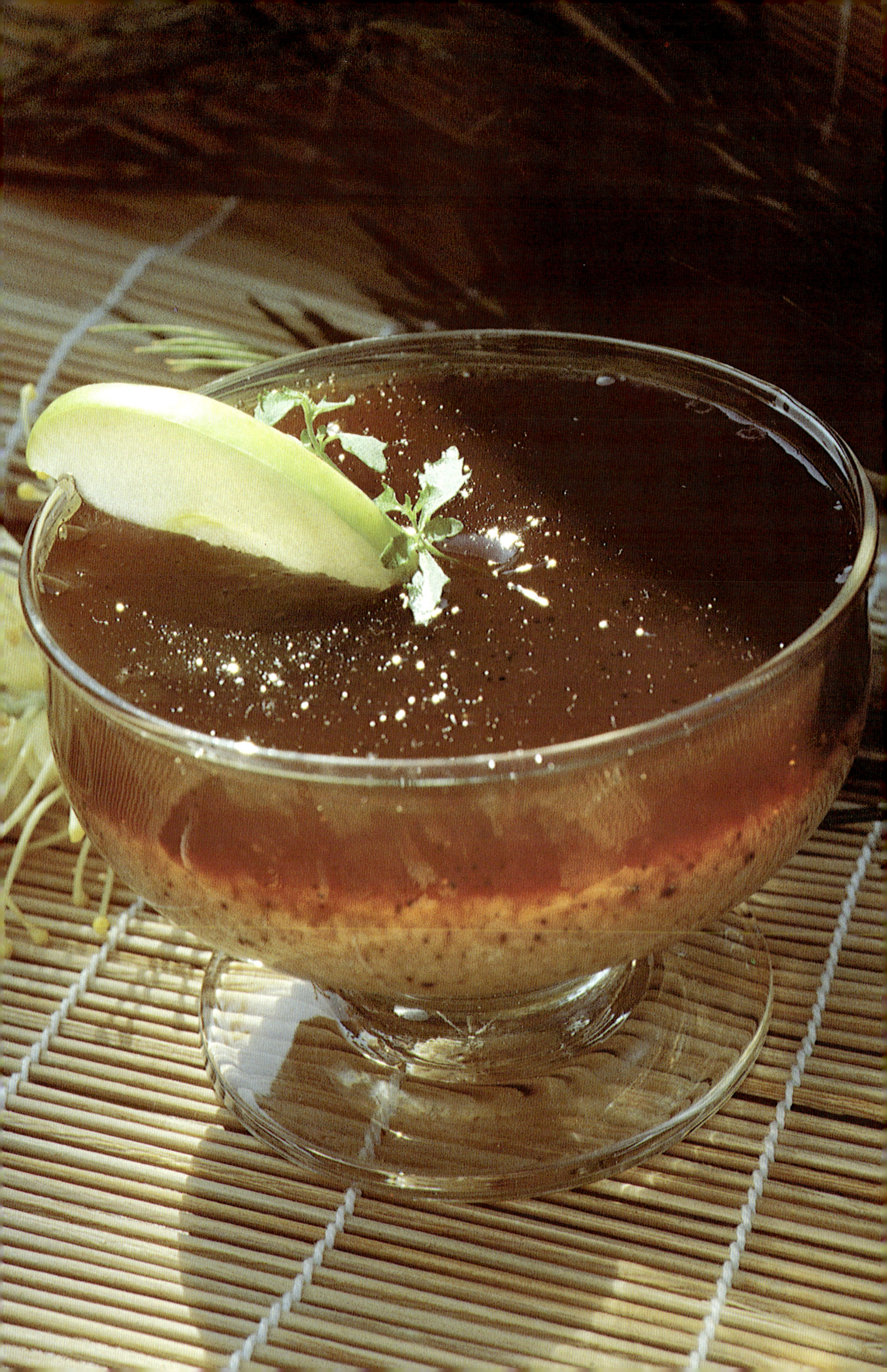

Munthari mousse

**6 tablespoons agar-agar flakes or 1 cup agar strips
2 cups fruit juice (apple or pear)
¼ cup maple syrup
1 egg white
2 tablespoons tahini
2 cups munthari berries**

Boil the agar-agar in the juice until it dissolves and allow the juice to cool a little then blend in the tahini and munthari. In a dry bowl, whip the egg white to stiff peaks and add the maple syrup. Fold the egg white into the fruit mixture. Pour into glasses and refrigerate. Garnish before serving.

Any native fruit can be used instead of the munthari. If the texture of agar agar is not to your liking use gelatine according to the manufacturers instructions for the volume of juice to set.

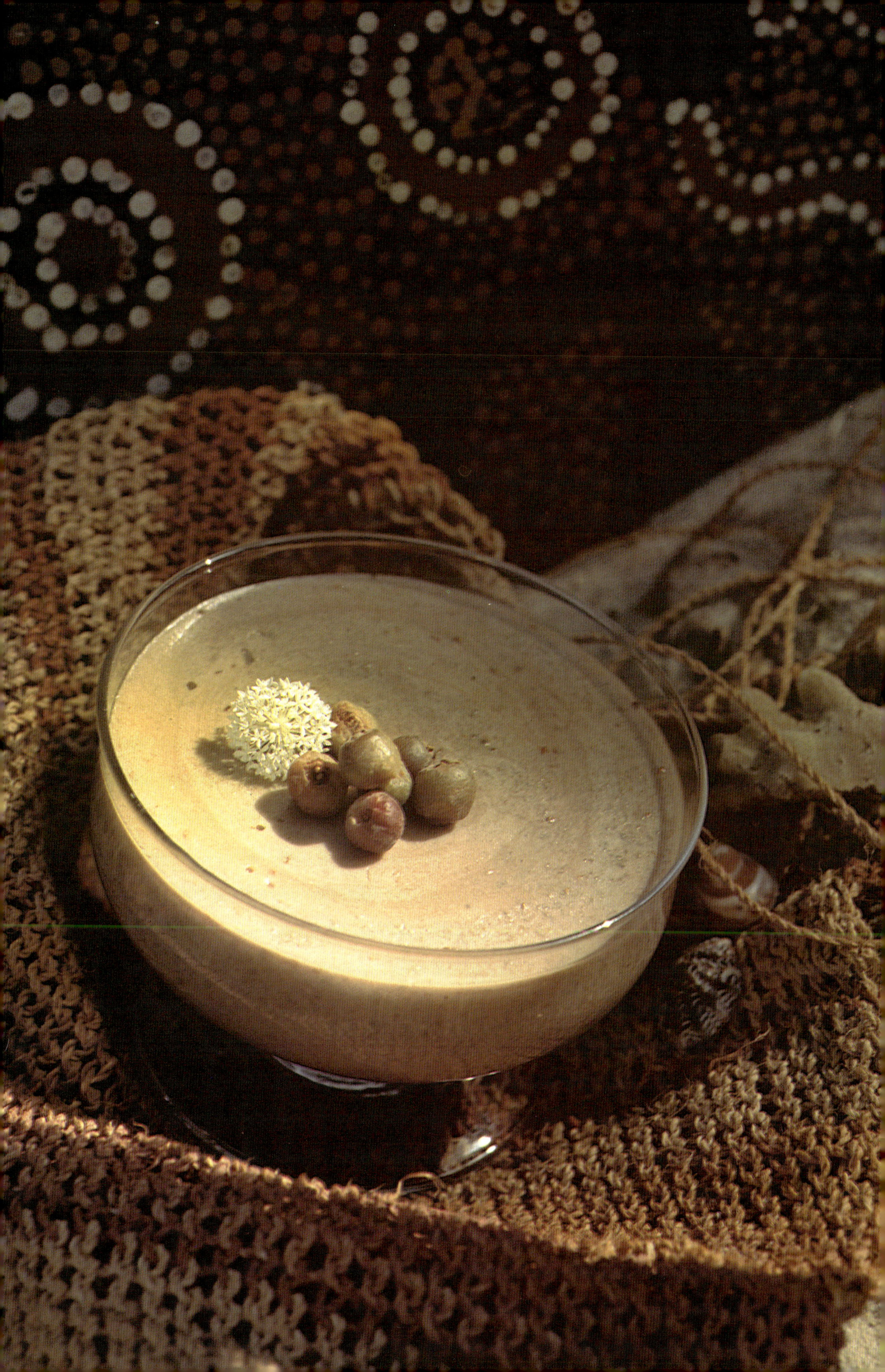

Native lime sago pudding

¼ cup sago pearls
1 cup cold water
2 oranges
8 to 10 native lime
¼ cup palm sugar (or to taste)
native mint for garnish

Add the sago to boiling water, stirring constantly to stop the sago from sticking. Cook until the sago balls are clear. Pour the sago into a sieve and wash with cold water. Drain. Juice the oranges and the native limes, reserving a few limes for garnishing. Dissolve the palm sugar in the juice and add to the sago. Pour into glasses and refrigerate before serving.

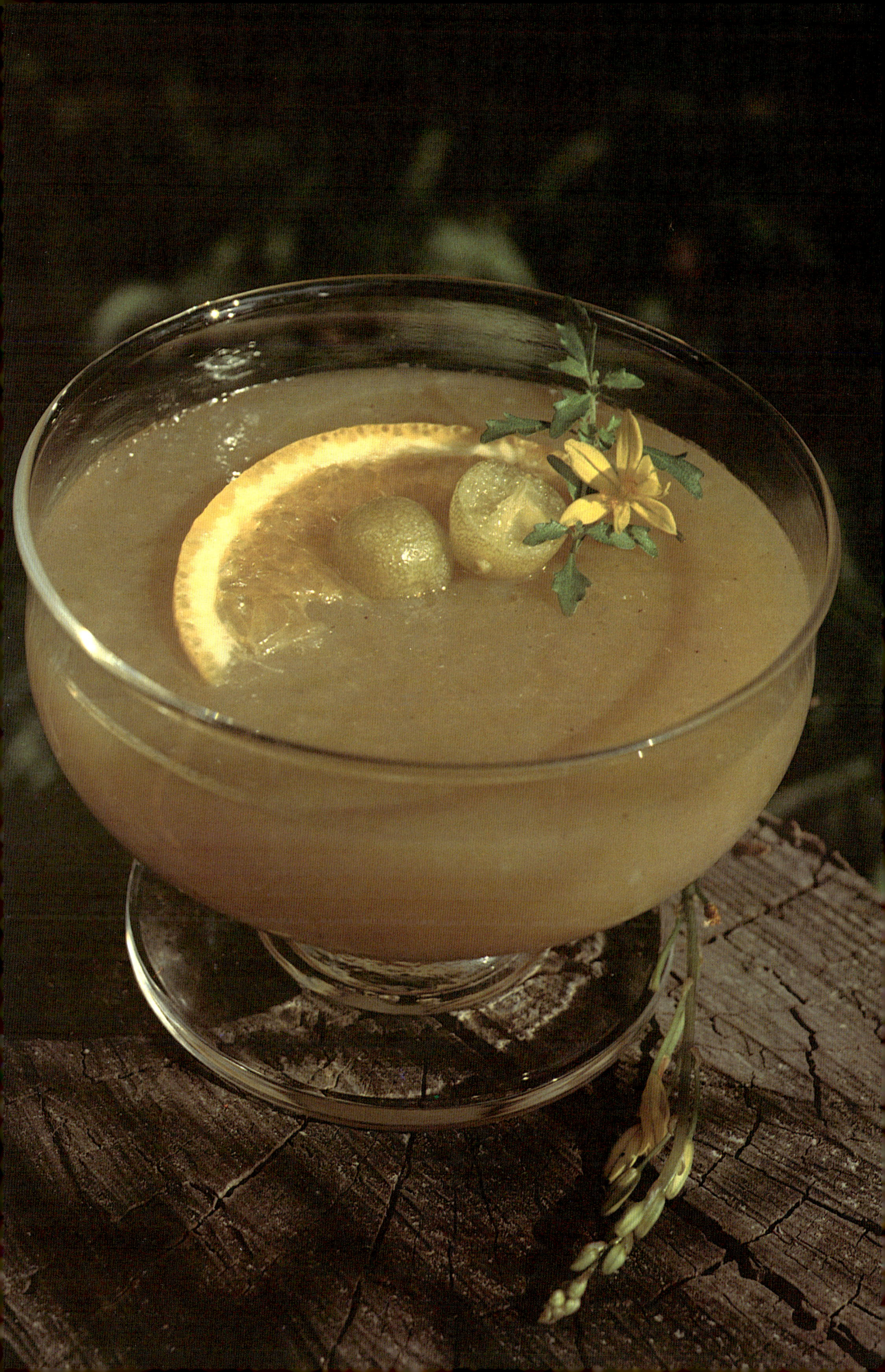

Uniquely Australian

Wattle truffles

Dipped truffles

**wattle filling
icing sugar
tempered chocolate**

Roll small amounts of the chilled wattle filling (see below) into balls using icing sugar to stop the filling from sticking to your hands. Dip each ball in tempered chocolate (see following overleaf), allow to set and then dip a second time. The chill of the cold filling will crack the first coat and the second coat fills these cracks and provides a little extra thickness. The trick in making an attractive dipped chocolate truffle is to twist and simultaneously invert the ball as it is pulled from the tempered chocolate. This wraps the chocolate tail around truffle and makes a swirled pattern on a smooth ball of chocolate.

Wattle filling

**300ml cream
1 tablespoon wattle
540g white couverture chocolate**

Bring the cream and wattle to the boil stirring constantly and pour over the chopped chocolate. Stir to a paste. Refrigerate the paste if making dipped truffles or else leave at room temperature for piping into the chocolate molds.

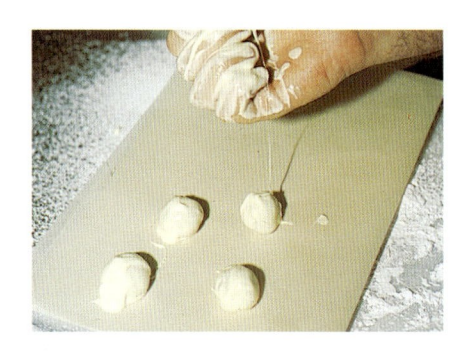

Store the chocolates in a cool dark place at a temperature no hotter than 18°C. The molded truffles tend to last longer than the dipped chocolates since the filling is not rolled in the hands and sterility can be maintained.

Wattle truffles

Molded truffles

**tempered chocolate
orange wattle syrup
wattle filling**

Pour tempered chocolate into a scrupulously clean chocolate mold and invert the mold to form the chocolate shell. Once the chocolate has set, pipe in the orange wattle syrup (see below) followed by the wattle filling which has been kept at room temperature. Fill the truffles to no more than 4mm from the top of the mold and finish with a sealing thickness of chocolate to form the base. Allow to set and shake the truffles from the mold. The chocolate should easily drop out from a clean mold but if they do not then place the mold into warm water without wetting the chocolates and shake again.

Orange wattle syrup

**60ml water
1 heaped teaspoon wattle
⅓ cup sugar
25ml orange liqueur**

Boil the water, wattle and sugar. Strain the essence into a double boiler or a microwave proof bowl. Boil or microwave on high power to reduce the essence to a thick syrup. Cool, then add the liqueur.

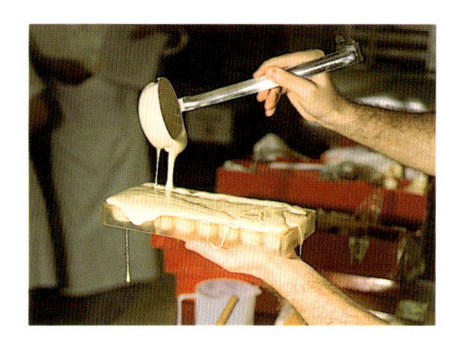

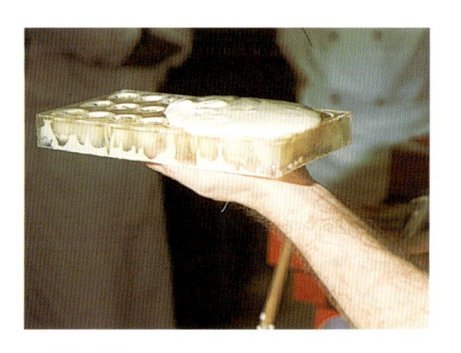

These chocolates can be served with a wattleccino for that perfect ending to a bushfood dinner. Similar wattle truffles are now being manufactured and exported to Japan and will no doubt become more available here in Australia.

Uniquely Australian

Tempering and dipping

Before chocolate can be used, it must be tempered. This process of bringing chocolate to temperature for use gives it the texture and set we expect of chocolate.

Over hot water, slowly melt the chocolate reaching a temperature of 40 to 50°C. Mix well to re-emulsify the fats and solids then cool to 26 to 32°C. The combined actions of mixing and cooling form the tempering. Tempering chocolate must be done quickly and without the addition of any other ingredients (for example, water would make the chocolate solidify beyond use). There are many ways to achieve temper. Chocolate may be tempered in a bowl sitting in cold water and stirred until the desired temperature is reached. Alternatively, the chocolate can be poured onto a clean marble slab (or other large cold surface) and mixed to cool. The tempered chocolate should then be kept at a temperature range of 26 to 32°C.

To test whether the temper has been achieved, drop some of the chocolate on a clean surface at room temperature. If it starts to set within 2 to 3 minutes it is ready to use. If it takes longer, it is too warm and needs to be cooled further.

Wattle chocolate truffles

Wattleccino ™

1 teaspoon wattle
soy or dairy milk

In a cappuccino machine prepare a cappuccino using no more than 1½ level teaspoons of wattle. The grounds expand with the heat and can block the hot water flow if too much is used. In addition, if the wattle is made too strong it will curdle the milk. Express ⅔ cup of wattle extract and add the frothed milk to fill the cup. A wattleccino makes an excellent bedtime drink since it is free of caffeine but also complements desserts and chocolates with its similarity to coffee but without the bitterness of coffee.

Try wattleccino without sweetener since the combination of milk and wattle imparts a sweet flavour. Wattle can also be prepared black or made very weak to be more like a tea.

Uniquely Australian

Black apple smoothie

**4 fully ripe black apples, seeds removed
250ml soy milk
maple syrup to taste**

Blend all the ingredients together and serve chilled or over ice.

Try making smoothies with munthari, stewed quandong or a few drops of eucalyptus oil and honey.

Bunya bunya nut and banana smoothie

**8 bunya nuts, boiled and shelled
1 over-ripe banana
250ml soy milk**

Blend all the ingredients together and serve chilled or over ice.

Try wattle, banana and maple syrup smoothies. Extract the wattle flavour by boiling a teaspoonful of wattle in ¼ cup of water. Add this to the soy milk and banana and blend well. Sweeten with honey or maple syrup if desired.

Most wild fruits vary in quality due to their wild character and genetic diversity. It is well worth trying fruits from different trees and making sure of the ripeness of the fruits. Many wild fruits do not reach maturity until they fall to the ground.

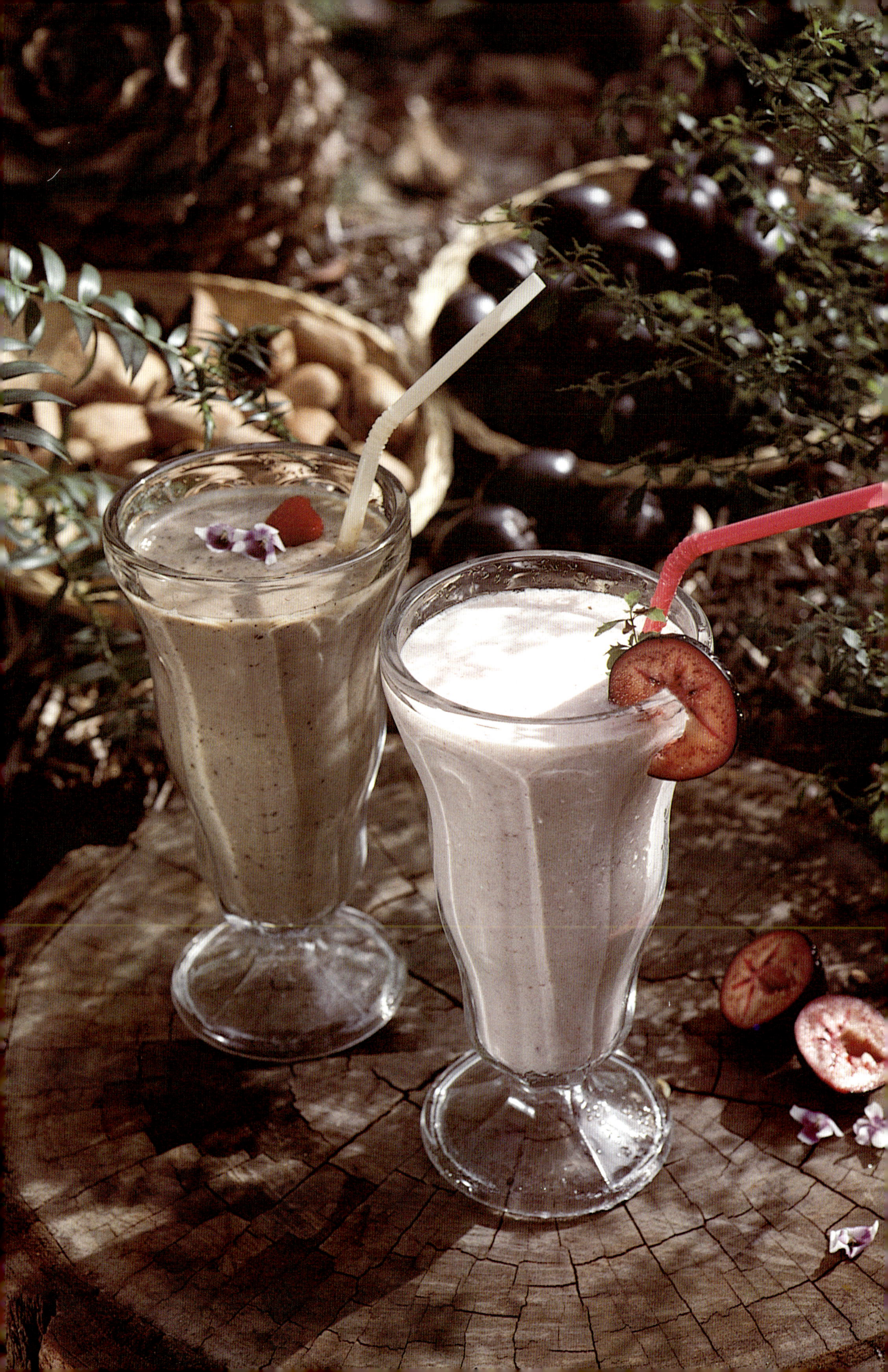

Uniquely Australian

Wild rosella cordial 1.

375g wild rosella flowers
1 cup lemon juice (strained)
250ml water
2 ½ cups sugar

Blend the rosella flowers briefly in a food processor to chop them. Bring all ingredients to the boil and simmer gently for 10 minutes. Skim frequently. Allow to cool then add a little cordial to a glass and top with water, mineral water or champagne.

Wild rosella cordial 2.

6 wild rosella flowers
5ml lemon aspen juice
5ml orange curacao
chilled champagne

Blend the rosella, lemon aspen juice and curacao until smooth. Strain into a champagne flute and top with champagne.

Wild rosella cordial 3.

10 wild rosella flowers
60ml apple juice
30ml native lime or 10ml lemon aspen juice
60ml chilled vodka

Blend to smoothness. Strain and serve.

The wild rosellas in this recipe are a part of the flowers of an introduced species of Hibiscus found growing wild in the Northern Territory. The bird with the same name does not make anywhere near as good a cordial.

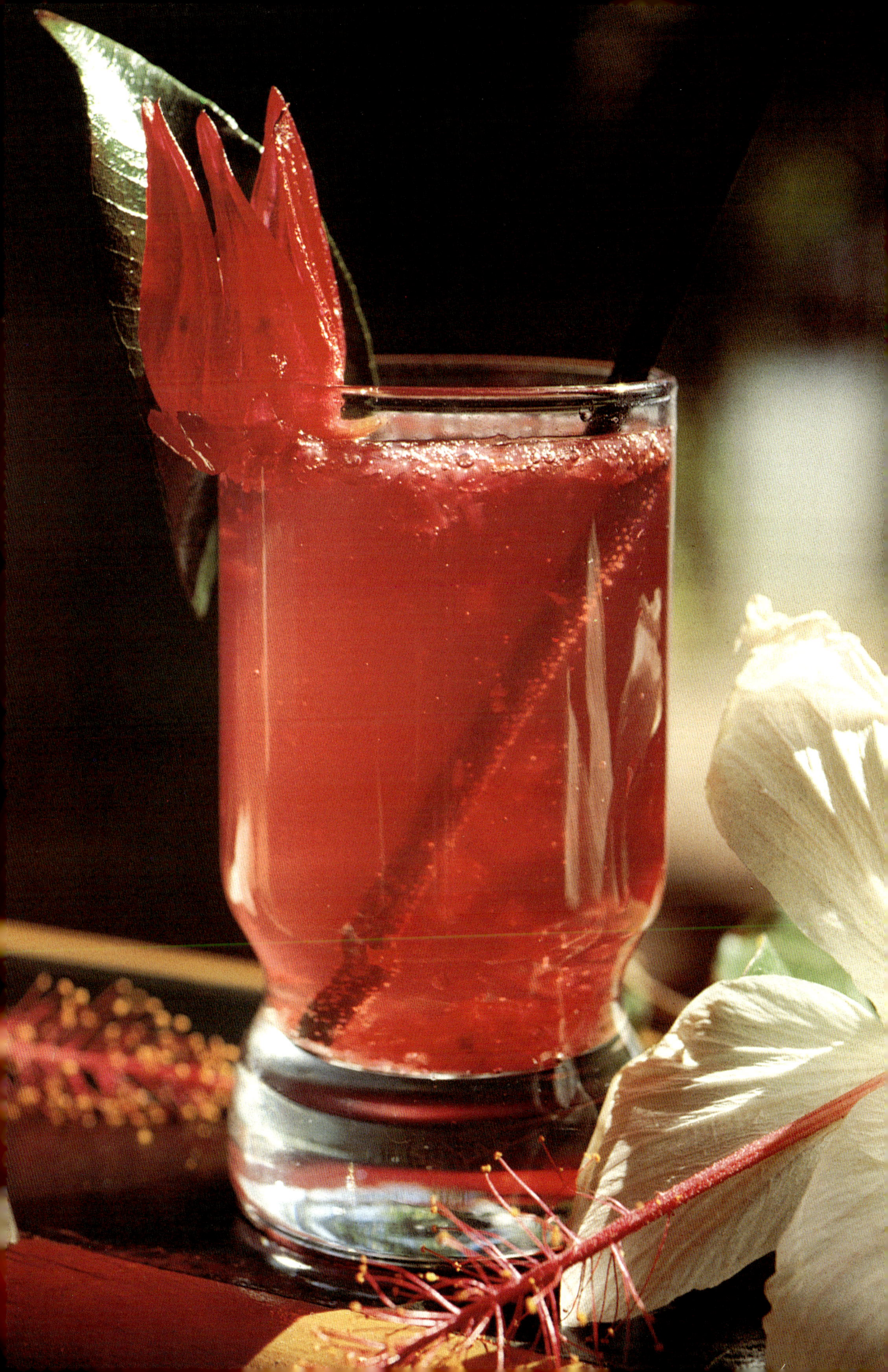

Rainforest punch

lemon aspen juice
whole rainforest fruits eg. riberries, midyim fruits
mineral water
apple juice

Mix the apple juice and mineral water in equal amounts. Add the lemon aspen juice to taste, try about a 5% addition. Toss in a few fruits and garnish with a sprig of native mint.

Rainforest punch with punch

45ml Bacardi rum
10ml lemon aspen juice
10ml maple syrup
ice

Blend all the ingredients and serve in a tall glass.

Native lime cocktail

30ml Bacardi rum
22ml Galliano
22ml Cointreau
22ml wild lime juice
ice

Pour all the ingredients into a cocktail shaker, shake then pour into a serving glass.

Wattle Irish cream

30ml Irish whiskey
120ml hot black wattle
fresh cream

Pour the whiskey into a serving glass and add the wattle. Carefully float the cream on the surface by pouring it into a spoon and letting it overflow onto the wattle.

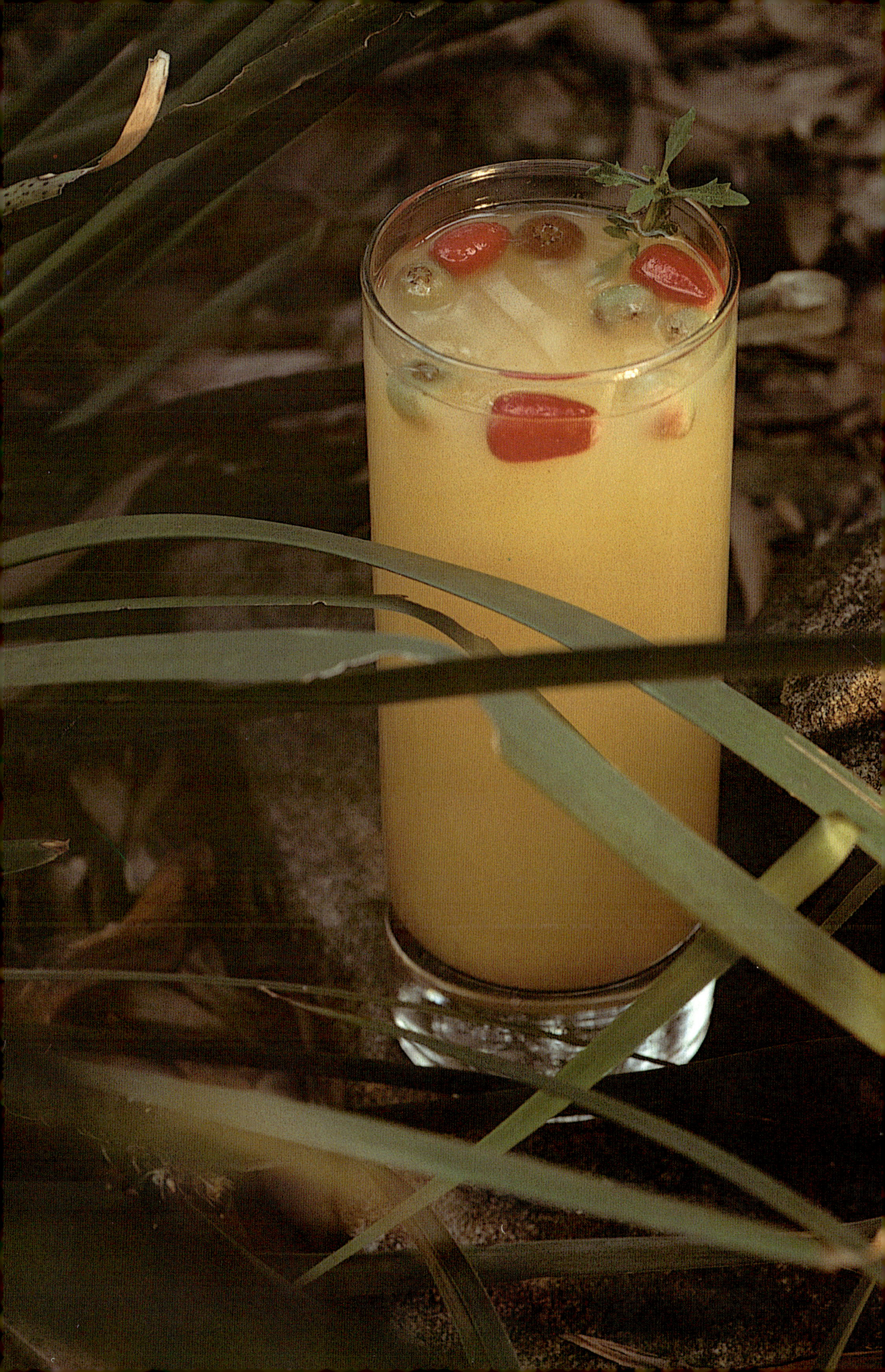

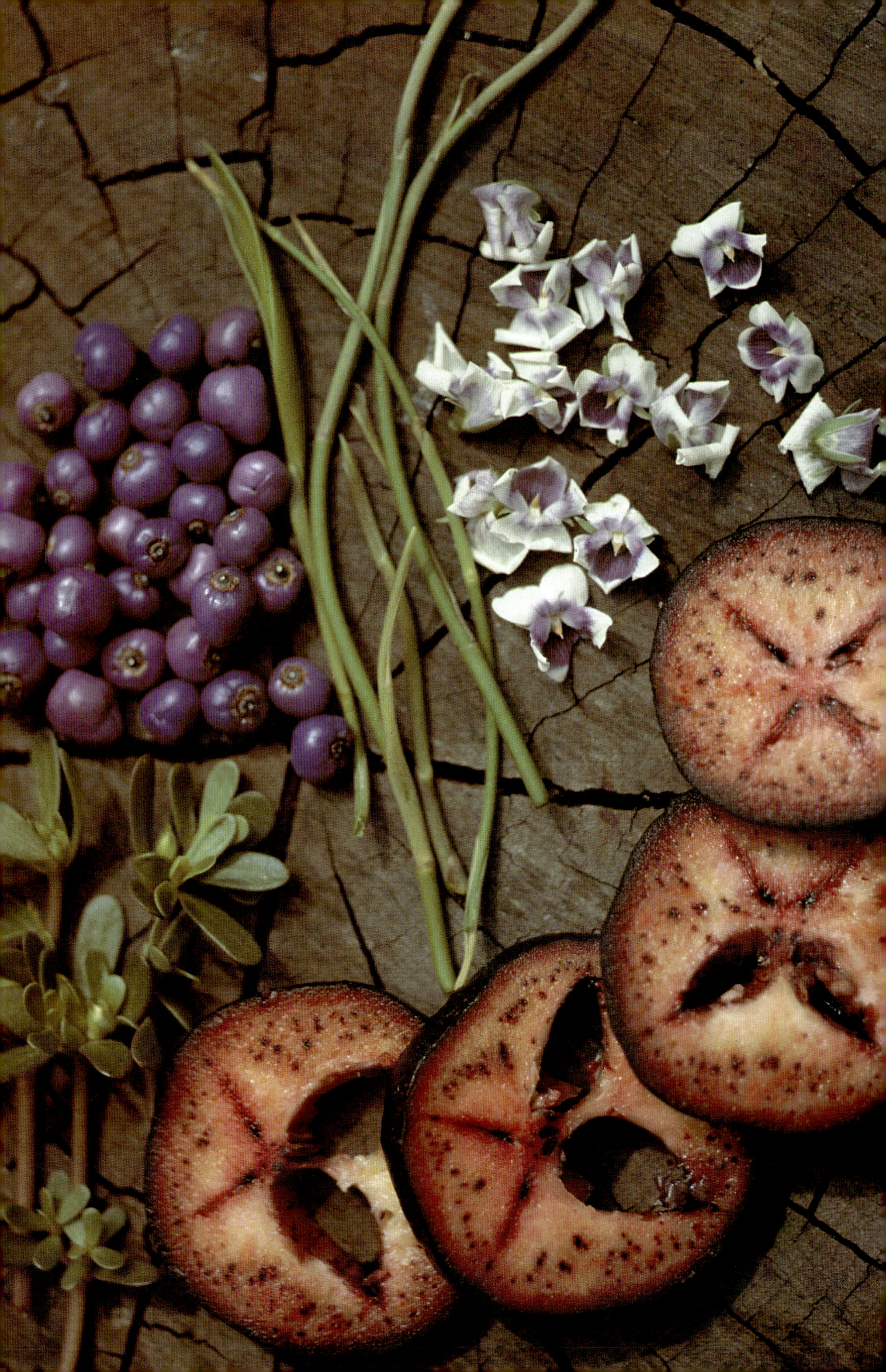

Uniquely Australian

Bushfood Glossary

The following section describes the bushfoods used in this book. Nearly all are commercially available, certainly in the major capital cities and further afield as supplies and demand grow. Some of the foods are even finding markets overseas. For more information on many of the foods refer to the Bush Food Handbook. For your local supplier, contact Bush Tucker Supply Pty Ltd in Sydney.

Apple berry or pudding fruit is a small forage food which has culinary applications but is not yet produced in sufficient quantities for marketing. The appleberry is ripe when it softens and turns a pale yellow colour.

The **black apple** is not an apple at all but the milky fruits of a large slow growing rainforest tree called Planchonella australis. The black apple and several of its edible relatives are found in remnant rainforest from the north coast of NSW up into north Queensland. The fruits have an apple, plum and custard character when they are at their best which is several days after they fall to the ground. The best way to 'cook' black apples is to freeze and then thaw them to soften the flesh. Heating makes the fruits become hard.

Black nightshade berries are edible once fully ripe and even the leaves have been used as a pot herb. The two common species are cosmopolitan plants found in urban areas along the east coast. They are often incorrectly called deadly nightshade but this name belongs to an introduced weed which is quite a different plant. The true deadly nightshade is called Atropa belladonna and is nowhere near as common as the black nightshades.

Black nightshade berries are best used as a garnish but will need to be foraged since they are not marketed commercially.

Bogong moths are a delicious insect to eat and were a staple of Aboriginal groups in the southern highlands of NSW and into Victoria. Like bacon, the moths need to be cooked to enhance their oily and nutty flavour.

Bunya bunya nuts are the large edible seeds from a native pine once only found in northern NSW and south east Qld but now widely planted from Victoria to the inland. Often likened to a chestnut in flavour, bunya nuts have nearly no fat or protein and are high in complex carbohydrates. These starches tend to lose moisture with storage but will re-hydrate on boiling. If the nut still has a dry centre after boiling and shelling then re-boil the nut meat only and complete the re-hydration.

There is a special knack to opening bunya bunya nuts. Boiling the nuts in their shells for at least 30 minutes will cook the nut as well as soften the shell. To cut the softened nut, use a towel to hold the hot nut and with a short, sharp knife pierce the shell with the knife tip. Lever the knife handle downwards, remove the knife and repeat the technique with the nut turned around 180° to the first cut. This will allow the nut to be removed in two halves leaving the red skin behind in the shell. Another method for shelling bunya nuts takes at least 4 or 5 hours but less effort. After boiling the nuts, leave them in the water to cool completely. As they cool the nuts will swell and crack their shells. Using a sharp knife again, the shells can be slit along the crack and the nuts removed whole. If the red skin covering he nut is difficult to remove with this technique, try bringing the water to the boil again before cutting the shells.

Use bunya nuts as garnishes, minced and cooked with soy milk or cream to make a wheat-free pastry or blend them with milk, cream, cooked semolina or ricotta cheese to make bunya purées of various consistencies. Cooking blended or minced bunya nuts hydrolyses the starches and thickens the mixture a little like cooking corn flour or arrowroot in custards and sauces. Bunya bunya nuts are a very versatile nut and their chestnut character allows them to be used in both sweet as well as savoury applications.

Burrawang flour: This is made from the highly carcinogenic seeds of a prehistoric palm. See the Bush Food Handbook for processing details. The flour is strenuously quality controlled and can be used as a flavouring for wheat flour. Burrawang flour has a yeasty cheese flavour which is particularly well suited to pasta and pancakes and dumpling doughs. TOXIC UNTIL PROCESSED

Bush cucumber is a new commercial species and is found on creek banks in dry country. The scrambling plant bears fruits which taste of a blend between the cultivated cucumber, melon and grape. The fruits are only small with a tough skin which needs to be removed before using the fruit as a garnish.

Bush tomatoes are wild Australian relatives of the tomato and potato. The species commonly available is harvested by Aborigines in Central Australia and one local language name is 'akudjura'. A bush tomato chutney is being manufactured commercially and a ground product is being developed and will be marketed as Akudjura. The fruits have a tamarillo-like flavour whole but ground into a powder they lose their slight bitterness and make a good substitute for a sweet paprika. The sprinkle is particularly good on fried onions or with cheeses and as a topping for savoury dishes.

Davidson's plum or sour plum lives up to its descriptive name but the red flesh and sharp tartness makes the large fruits very well suited to dressings, sauces and desserts. The acidity of Davidson's plum complements fatty foods particularly well.

Uniquely Australian

Dianella berries make an unusual garnish due to their bright purple colour. They are being grown in Enrichland Polyculture systems and are becoming commercially available.

Dodder laurel fruits are an interesting forage food with a unique flavour. The sticky seed in each fruit can be removed from the opening at the bottom of the fruit leaving the flesh intact. Dodder laurel is a parasitic plant and is not yet grown as a commercial species.

Emu is now being farmed in several Australian states and should become more popular as the market grows. The meat is red not white as commonly expected and is available as foresaddle, hindsaddle and drum with the hindsaddle providing the best steaks. Both saddles produce an exceptional cold smoked meat. The drum is best suited for the manufacture of smallgoods. Other products from emus include offal, leather, oil, claws and feathers. The eggs are equivalent to around ten chicken eggs and can taste a little rich or gamey when first opened. This game flavour lessens on standing.

Eucalyptus oil (food grade) The characteristically Australian flavoured oil is distilled from the leaves of a range of gum trees then specially re-distilled to separate the edible fraction from other toxic oil components. Most eucalyptus oil is produced overseas from plantation gums. When using eucalyptus oil as a food flavouring do not taste for strength too often since the strong flavour tends to deaden the taste buds. Eat something else and come back to the eucalyptus later. The eucalyptus should be a subtle after taste and not a distinctive flavour. Be sure to use food grade oil and not the eucalyptus oil more generally available.

The **Illawarra plum** or brown pine plum is an east-coast rainforest tree. The fruit has an external seed and the edible portion is the swollen stem. It has a plum character with a hint of pine and a sticky texture. The Illawarra plum is a difficult fruit to use due to its tendency to go bitter. To minimise the risk of bitterness avoid using under-ripe fruit or over-cooking. When taste testing sauces or jams do not try them hot. The bitterness often disappears on cooling and do not use aluminium cookware. Once mastered, the use of Illawarra plums in sauces and fruit blends produces incomparable results. Classic products are Illawarra plum and chilli sauces, fresh fruit compote, glacéed plums and Illawarra plum jam.

Kangaroo and wallaby meat are becoming increasingly available as Australians slowly learn to value and properly manage their natural resources. Wallaby meat is processed in Tasmania while kangaroo meat for human consumption is dominated by production from South Australia. Other States are soon to enter the market and the export of kangaroo meat is set to expand dramatically.

All game animal muscle meats are low in fat and rich in protein and iron. The proportion of poly-unsaturated fat to total fat is higher than with domesticated animals. However, the fat content could change if the animals are inappropriately farmed and their wild quality diminishes. Passive rearing, that is, the culling of managed populations is the preferred and most humane farming method for all our native animals suitable for meat production.

Several kangaroo meat products are available including a cold smoked backstrap fillet flavoured with native pepper. Smallgoods are also in production and popular products are gourmet sausages and a kangaroo pepperoni, marketed in South Australia as Pepperooni™

Kakadu plum is the new marketing name for the green or billy goat plum which is an olive sized fruit from Australia's tropical north and the world's highest fruit source of vitamin C. The fruit pickles well and is commercially manufactured into a jelly. It has been the focus of attention overseas because of its vitamin content and may soon be developed in Europe as a flavouring and natural vitamin source before much is done here in Australia.

The **kangaroo apple** is a member of the tomato family. The plants are shrubs or small trees but the fruits of some varieties can be too seedy to be useful for culinary use. Some selection is necessary to encourage the development of the small seeded forms. Kangaroo apples are widespread with good varieties common throughout the plants' range.

Kurrajong flour is made from the roasted and ground seeds of a range of trees called kurrajongs which includes the common Illawarra flame tree. All kurrajong seeds are edible only after roasting and are high in fat, protein, carbohydrate and fibre. The flour adds a nutty flavour to breads, pastries, dumplings and crumbs as well as a tasty oily character similar to a blend of roasted peanuts and Brazil nuts. Kurrajong flour makes an interesting spread with macadamia nut oil or mixed into tahini. The name, kurrajong, is from the Aboriginal language of the Dhurak people who lived in the Sydney region.

Lemon aspen is a rainforest fruit found along the eastern coast of Australia and has one of the most interesting bushfood flavours. The small yellow fruit has a strong citrus tang but tastes unlike any conventional citrus. The juice is very versatile and is a good replacement for lemon juice in most applications. Store the juice in the refrigerator and it will keep for months. Freeze any pulp leftover from preparing the juice for future use as a shortbread flavouring or for making cordials or cocktails.

Lemon myrtle leaves are similar in taste to a blend of the oils in a sweet lemon grass, lemon leaves and lime leaves. The variety of lemon myrtle sold commercially has been analysed and contains very low levels of any harmful essential oils. Other varieties may not be so 'sweet'. The leaves can be used fresh or dried. Depending upon the recipe, use an infusion of whole leaves, shred fresh leaves or grind dry leaves to a powder in an electric coffee grinder or a mortar and pestle. Lemon myrtle makes an excellent herb butter or can be baked into breads.

Lemon-scented tea tree is a condiment plant used to impart a lemon flavour into fish when cooking in paperbark. Not recommended as a tea due to its content of citronella oils.

Lemon tea tree is another lemon flavoured herb tree but a citronella-free form of a species found in swamps on the north coast of New South Wales is being grown and wild harvested in limited quantities. Lemon tea tree makes an excellent herb tea and food flavouring.

Midyim berry. These tiny berries are an excellent garnish and forage food. The small white spotted fruits have an apple and ginger flavour but are not yet available commercially.

Munthari are small, fragrant, apple-flavoured berries from a beach creeper common on dunes in southern South Australia. Also called muntries, emu apples or native cranberries munthari can be used in sauces, pies or eaten just as they come. A freeze-dried product may soon be available as a snack food.

Mushrooms. There are many native edible fungi including puffballs, morels, inkcaps, boletes and bracket fungi. Identification prior to consumption is absolutely essential to maintain a healthy liver. Poisonous fungi can be extremely toxic with enough mushroom to just cover the nail of your smallest finger being sufficient to stop liver function entirely. Once identified as edible, wild mushrooms offer a range of interesting flavours usually stronger and more earthy than cultivated mushrooms.

All puffballs are edible when they are completely white inside. Pan-fry slices in butter but cut them very thinly since their flavour is often very intense.

Uniquely Australian

Native aniseed leaves are harvested from a rare plant originally found in north coast New South Wales and south-east Queensland rainforests. The commercially available native aniseed leaves are only harvested from artificially propagated plants and is still very limited in availability. Use native aniseed in a similar fashion to lemon myrtle leaves.

Native currants are the sour green fruits of a parasitic shrub growing in woodland areas from the Great Dividing Range to the coast. Native currants make a delicious ice cream.

Native gooseberry fruits are a smaller native version of the Cape Gooseberry but have a similar taste and appearance. Common on beaches in the Top End and widespread along the coast, the native gooseberry will grow well in Sydney and is being developed as a commercial species.

Native limes are fruits of several species of indigenous citrus usually found in dry rainforests or arid areas. The most popular native lime is the small but juicy, yellow lime found in south-east Queensland.

Native mint is harvested from two of our native mintbush species. The flavour is very strong and builds up with time when incorporated into sauces, pesto, bunya nut butters or vinegars.

Native pepper leaves are harvested from a range of small shrubs and trees found in Tasmania, Victoria and New South Wales. Flavours from each of three species vary from a gum-like character to a banana pepper and with different amounts of zing. As supplies firm, the native pepper now available in quantity will be marketed as Mountain pepper. The other two species will be called Snow pepper and Dorrigo pepper.

Native violet flowers make an appealing garnish but need to be picked as fresh as possible and dropped into cold water so as not to wilt. Set them in jellies for that special dessert.

Paperbark is a useful natural biodegradable material which can replace greaseproof paper, baking paper, oven bags, plastic wrap and aluminium foil. Paperbark imparts a delicate smoke flavour which is particularly noticeable with poultry or freshwater fish. Vegetables can also be wrapped and baked in paperbark and the whole package served at the table. Line platters with paperbark for finger food served Aboriginal style.

Portulaca is a cosmopolitan plant common in urban areas. The leaves and stems can be used after blanching as an interesting salad green. Aborigines milled the tiny black and oily seeds to a flour but our technology makes hard work of this hard seed producing a gritty, almost unusable seedmeal.

Quandong is an Aboriginal word of the Wiradhuri people who lived in south-west N.S.W. Quandongs are sometimes called native peaches but the fruits have a flavour which is more like a blend of a tart apricot and peach. Quandongs are well known to country folk for making jam or using in pies and were often dried for storage. They are available fresh, frozen and dried.

Samphire is a low growing plant found in mangrove and estuary mudflat communities. Samphire is related to similar plants in Europe and is being used to reclaim salt-affected agricultural land in Victoria. The salty, fleshy but leafless stems need to be steamed or blanched to remove an astringency which makes the raw stems inedible. Samphire makes an excellent pickle on its own or in combination with other bushfoods and herbs.

Scrambling lily stem tips are a delicious substitute for asparagus and the lily is a highly commercial species when grown under Enrichland Polyculture. The tips can be eaten raw and do not need any processing.

Sugarbag is a widely used colloquial Aboriginal-English name for the honey from native bees. The name came from the comparison to the white bushman's sugar which always came in a bag. At least two species of native bee, *Trigona carbonaria* and *T. australis*, form colonies in hollow trees, in rock crevices and in northern Australia, in termite mounds. *T. carbonaria* is the more common and can be found all along the east coast and well inland. Native bees are found all over Australia except in parts of the arid centre. Here Aborigines harvested honey ants, gum exudates and lerp as their sweet foods. Recently, artificial hives have been designed to successfully house native bees. These hives can be designed as breeding boxes which are easily split when full. Alternatively, a honey chamber can be added to the top of the hive and honey harvested each year. Bees in the warmer climates may make up to a litre of honey each year, whereas in Sydney the bees only go out to gather nectar once the temperature goes over 18 to 20°C. Southern bees thus have shorter working hours and probably harvest nectar at a slower pace than bees in the tropics and sub-tropics.

This production from native hives may be very small by comparison to the feral European bee but the quality of the honey is high. The taste of sugarbag from *Trigona carbonaria* can be described as bitter-sweet with the mellowness of a smooth port wine and a pleasant, resinous character. By comparison, a species which is common in northern Australia, *Trigona*

Uniquely Australian

australis, makes honey which is almost identical in flavour to big bee honey. The flavour and colour of all native bee honey will also vary depending upon what plant species are in flower and which tree kinos and resins are being harvested as well. Many of the flavour components are volatile and can evaporate if the honey is heated. On hot toast or even on a hot day, the flavour can disappear. The best applications for sugarbag are therefore, in chilled desserts particularly with dairy or soy milk cream which accent the delicate qualities of the honey. Try making a sugarbag butter by whipping sugarbag into slightly softened butter or into low-fat ricotta cheese. Do not forget about the best application for sugarbag: Like a good port, sugarbag is always at its best just sipped and enjoyed as it comes.

Out in the bush, Aborigines still seek out wild hives and attribute a tonic quality to the honey which contains slow release carbohydrates, waxes and pollen proteins. Unfortunately, in cities and around towns, bushland tends to be burnt often. Hollow trees which provide homes for native bee hives are quick to burn and very slow to be replaced. Keeping native bees in artificial hives can therefore, be ecologically beneficial. European bees appear to be affecting the species composition of native plant communities and could well be called feral floral pigs. Look at any flowering plant for an idea of just how many floral pigs are around. In heathland, many tubular flowers are being raided by European bees. They get at the nectar by biting the back of the flower avoiding the pollinating mechanism. (The floral pigs are usually too big to fit down the tiny bell shaped flowers). While robbing the nectar, the big bee leaves a chemical repellant called a pheremone, perhaps to mark the flower as 'visited, don't call again, today'. This pheremone repels the flowers' native pollinators, the plant never produces seed and the species eventually disappear. Little bees do not seem to exhibit this anti-social behaviour and are well suited to pollinating many native flowers. They are also eaten by native birds which does not seem to be a problem in terms of maintaining hives but just adds to the web of life. We are all food for some living thing.

Water chestnuts. The native Australian species of water chestnuts is the same as that grown in Asia and is a favourite Aboriginal food. It is found in the swamps of Arnhemland and other parts of the Top End of tropical Australia. Water chestnuts are now cultivated as far south as Brisbane. Fresh or frozen, roasted water chestnuts are a sweet substitute for baby potatoes and can be cooked whole and unskinned. Simply remove any remains of the rootbundle and stalk.

Warrigal greens is the new marketing name for a wild spinach found around mangroves along the coast and along the banks of inland rivers. Warrigal greens harvested in New Zealand (NZ spinach) were used by Captain Cook in the 1770s in his battle against scurvy. Another name acquired on the Sydney leg of Cook's trip was Botany Bay greens and their use was recorded in the Endeavour's diaries. Collections of warrigal greens have found their way to the Kew Botanic Gardens in the U.K. and then out to the back blocks of Paris, France where it now grows as an urban weed. Warrigals are harvested by Parisiennes and is known as Tetragon and preferred over English spinach.

Wattle This is the second commercialised native plant species, only following the macadamia into production by 100 years. Wattle is made from the roasted seeds of one species of the thousand wattles found in Australia and is harvested by Aborigines west of the Great Dividing Range. The product is slowly becoming famous for its versatility as well as its Australian nature. It is currently used as a flavouring for ice-cream, pasta, chocolates, biscuits, bread and as a beverage (cf wattleccino).

Wild oranges are better called orange mustard fruits because of their peppery character. The seedy fruits are best used as a spice rather than trying to be guided by its common name.

Wild raspberries can be stunningly flavoured, particularly those grown in semi-shade. Even the leaves can be infused for their delicate raspberry taste. The plants are not yet cultivated but some varieties have a good potential.

Wild rosella for culinary use is not the bird but a brilliant red, flower-like fruit case with an acid-crisp taste. The edible portion consists of the petals and sepals of the fertilised flower from a naturalised weed in the Hibiscus family. Native rosellas are usually white or yellow and do not have the acid flavour of the weed.

Wild tamarinds are acid tasting and brilliantly coloured yellow, orange or red fruits from several different species of rainforest trees. The part used is called an aril and is well suited to sauces, dressings and desserts.

Witjuti grubs are the larvae of Cossid moths which include hawk and wood moths. These often lay their eggs in specific species of wattles and witjuti bush is one particular wattle harbouring witjuti grubs. Other grubs can be found in river red gums and are equally tasty to the true witjuti grub of Central Australia.

Yams are the tubers of a twining vine with heart-shaped leaves. They are mainly tropical but are rarely cultivated due to their short shelf life. Yams generally have a chewy texture and are high in dietary fibre and as such, are very nutritious. They are an ideal species to grow at home and foraged at the end of autumn or early winter.

Recipe index

Aussie bush bomb   126
Barramundi with muntharies   80
Barramundi out bush   32
Beach camp crab soup   30
Beef tenderloin with quandong   110
Black apple flan   144
Black apple smoothie   182
Bogong moth toasts   46
Buffalo and native mint burgers   66
Bunya nut and banana smoothie   182
Bunya nut ice cream with sugarbag   150
Bunya nut pudding   130
Bunya nut and pumpkin soup   44
Bunya nut smoked mutton salad   114
Bunya nut torte 1.   146
Bunya nut torte 2.   148
Bunya nut vegetarian pie   90
Bunya nut and wattle cream   134
Burrawang bread   46
Bush fired water buffalo tenderloin   106
Bush tomato soup   40
Capretto goat with a native pepperleaf sauce   104
Chocolate and wattle mousse   122
Clay rack of lamb   94
Cobra or mangrove worm   25
Cooking in a ground oven   34
Corn, myrtle and lime soup   43
Crocodile and wattle burgers   66
Crocodile chargrill   88
Eel spread   46
Emu burgers   66
Emu egg quiche   50
Fish fries   32
Goanna   28
Illawarra plum and bush tomato sauce   64
Illawarra plum cheesecake and rosella sauce   149
Illawarra plum and riberry tart   158
Johnny cakes   29
Kangaroo broth and kurrajong dumplings   118

Kangaroo burgers 66
Kangaroo fillet with quandong chilli sauce 98
Kangaroo quiche 50
Kangaroo stew under a kurrajong crust 38
Kurrajong and spice focaccia 58
Lamb cutlet duet 112
Lamb loin with bunya nuts and warrigal greens 100
Lemon aspen butter sauce 76
Lemon aspen curd 156
Lemon aspen curd tarlets 160
Lemon aspen ice cream 142
Lemon myrtle bavarois 154
Lemon myrtle and billy tea sorbet 128
Macadamia nut cream 158
Macadamia nut ice cream 140
Macadamia nut and warrigal greens 64
Marinated kangaroo kurrajong 102
Marron with macadamia nut and native lime mayonnaise 82
Miner's fruit bag 132
Mini pizzas 41
Moreton Bay bugs 'Eumundi' 78
Moreton Bay bugs on kurrajong pancakes 72
Munthari mousse 174
Munthari muffins 138
Mushroom soup 44
Native herb vinegars 42
Native lime cocktail 186
Native lime mayonnaise 82
Native lime sago pudding 176
Native mint salad 64
Nyngan mud cake 152
Paperbark baked lamb with bunya nut purée and wild fruit chutney 116
Pasta 60
Pickled native plums 74
Polenta slice 54
Prawn and ginger soup 38
Prawns on a wattle pancake 84
Quandong chilli sauce 98
Quandong pie with lemon aspen ice cream 142
Rainbow trout and seafood 87
Rainforest breads 164

Rainforest punch   186
Rainforest punch with punch   186
Riberry bread and butter pudding   124
Riberry jelly   170
Riberry muffins   166
Riberry quail   96
Roasted witjuti grubs   46
Rolled wattle and bunya nut pavlova   134
Sardines in macadamia nut oil   74
Seared emu medallions   102
Soused Coorong mullet with munthari   70
Smoked emu   108
Smoked game, ratatouille and salad   48
Stingray on coals   26
Stuffed vegetables   52
Shellfish in sand   24
Snake   28
Thumbprint cookies   168
Vegetarian lasagne   92
Warrigal green roulade   56
Warrigal green soup   44
Warrigal salad   48
Wattle and bunya focaccia   58
Wattleccino   181
Wattle cones with macadamia nut ice cream   140
Wattle Irish cream   186
Wattle jelly cups   172
Wattle pancakes with lemon aspen curd   156
Wattle sauce   130
Wattle truffles   178
Wild fruit chutney   116
Wild rosella cordial 1, 2 and 3.   184
Wild rosella mousse cake   136
Wild rosella and native currant tartlets   162
Wild rosella and tamarind sauce   132
Witjuti grub dip   46
Yabbies and whiting with lemon aspen butter   76
Yabby ravioli   62

Ingredient index

Aniseed myrtle   42, 58, 74, 87, 164
Barramundi   32, 80
Beef   110
Black apple   116, 144, 182
Black nightshade   53
Bogong moths   46
Buffalo   66, 106
Bunya bunya nuts   44, 53, 54, 88, 90, 100, 116, 130, 134, 146, 148, 149, 150, 182
Burrawang flour   46, 60, 62
Bush honey   see sugarbag
Bush tomato   38, 40, 41, 50, 53, 58, 60, 64, 92, 110
Clams   24
Cobra   see mangrove worm
Cockles   24
Crocodile   66, 88
Eel   46
Emu   48, 66, 102, 108
Emu egg   50
Eucalyptus oil   see gumleaf oil
File snake   28
Finned fish   26, 32, 70, 74, 76, 80, 87
Goanna   28
Goat   104
Gumleaf oil   80, 94, 108, 114, 126
Honey   164, 166
Illawarra plum   64, 74, 116, 132, 149
Kakadu plum   74, 102
Kangaroo   38, 48, 50, 98, 102, 118
Kangaroo apple   53
Kumara   52, 90
Kurrajong flour   38, 58, 72, 102, 112, 118
Lamb   94, 100, 112, 114, 116
Lemon aspen   62, 72, 74, 76, 87, 114, 116, 122, 142, 149, 156, 160, 184, 186
Lemon myrtle   42, 43, 58, 74, 80, 102, 118, 128, 154, 164
Lemon tea tree   42, 87, 112, 118
Macadamia nut   52, 53, 54, 64, 82, 112, 124, 134, 140, 158, 162. 164, 168, 170
Macadamia nut oil   46, 48, 58, 62, 64, 72, 74, 78, 82, 84, 88, 90, 94, 96, 98, 102, 104, 106, 108, 112, 166, 168
Mangrove worm   25

Uniquely Australian

Marron   82
Midyim   186
Moreton Bay bugs   72, 78
Mountain pepper   see native pepperleaf
Mudcrab   26, 30
Mullet   70
Munthari   53, 70, 80, 102, 132, 138, 174
Mussels   24
Mutton   see lamb
Native aniseed   see aniseed myrtle
Native currants   162
Native gooseberries   48
Native leeks   50, 53, 64, 118
Native limes   43, 82, 84, 108, 122, 176, 186, 188
Native mint   53, 64, 66, 116, 144, 176
Native pepperleaf   30, 38, 44, 50, 52, 53, 54, 56, 58, 62, 66, 102
Native violet flowers   48, 53
Nerites   26
Paperbark   87, 116
Pippies   24
Prawns   38, 84, 87
Quandong   98, 102, 110, 132, 142
Rainforest celery   42
Riberries   96, 118, 124, 132, 158, 164, 166, 168, 170, 186
Rosella   106, 132, 136, 149, 162, 184
Seafood   26, 30, 32, 38, 62, 70, 72, 74, 76, 78, 80, 82, 84, 87
Shark   26
Shellfish   24, 25, 26, 30, 38, 62, 72, 76, 78, 82, 84, 87
Snake   28
Stingray   26
Sugarbag   116, 126, 131, 138, 150, 164
Vongoles   26
Warrigal greens   30, 44, 48, 50, 53, 56, 60, 64, 84, 87, 90, 100, 106
Water chestnut   148
Wattle or wattleseed   58, 60, 66, 78, 84, 88, 112, 122, 126, 130, 134, 140, 144, 152, 156, 164, 168, 172, 178, 179, 181, 186
Whiting   76
Witjuti grubs   46
Yabbies   62, 76

Uniquely Australian

Menu ideas

Entrées

Oysters Van Dieman (topped with Tasmanian brie and pepperberries)

Smoked emu and quandong kernel yoghurt on wattle blini

Cold-cured roo on mountain pepper damper slices with outback fruit chutney

Barralax with a lemon myrtle oil finish

Gumleaf gravalax curls filled with garlic cream cheese

Paperbark-baked baby barramundi with Kakadu plum slices

Grilled prawns with warrigal greens on native mint fettuccine

Poached pears stuffed with akudjura tapinade, wrapped with emu proscuitto and drizzled with a cheesefruit cream

Leek and potato soup with bush bread and wild herb oil

Mains

Kangaroo fillet with mountain pepper and pepperberry sauce

Grilled Northern Territory buffalo tenderloin and a quandong chilli jus

Ilambo lamb stuffed with bunya nut Doongara rice and native thyme

Tandoori chicken filled with a wattle and macadamia nut mousseline

Beef fillet grill under a riberry jus and wattle and potato rosti

New season lamb rack with Illawarra and Davidson's plum port wine sauce

Veal fillet, aniseed myrtle mustard pear and wilted warrigal greens

Rib of beef, glazed bunya nuts and wattle and red wine sauce

Roast turkey with munthari jam and a macadamia nut and lime sauce

John Dory in a paperbark wrap with native mint and peppermint seasonings

Uniquely Australian

Desserts

Lemon myrtle bavarois garnished with a honey soaked lemon aspen rosella flower

Munthari bread and butter pudding and a wattle cream

Native peppermint mousse with Kakadu plum jelly

Mountain pepper pineapple with aniseed myrtle ice cream and wild lime glaze

Apple and quandong strudel under a quandong kernel creme fraiche

Frozen wattleccino and gumleaf honey

Lemon myrtle honey syrup drizzled over a wild fruit pudding

Wattle pancake stack and maple riberry cream

Granite of lemon aspen and almond crush

Munthari and apricot pie

Bush fruit and herb Xmas pudding and myrtle cream

Wattle tiramisu

Sweet lemon myrtle fettuccine and glacéed riberries

Illawarra plum wine trifle

Wild lime souffle with foamy brandy

Quandong liqueur tart

Aniseed myrtle butter and custard cake

Native flavoured chocolates and bunya nut chews

Mountain pepper and quandong ice cream with poached pears

Wild fruit blancmange with deep-fried bunya nut purée

Poached fresh figs with munthari creme anglaise

Wattle or native herb teas

Other bushfood recipes

Other bushfood recipes

Other bushfood recipes